Philip A. Marquam

The Saviour's Bible

A Divine Revelation

Philip A. Marquam

The Saviour's Bible
A Divine Revelation

ISBN/EAN: 9783337780166

Printed in Europe, USA, Canada, Australia, Japan

Cover: Foto ©Lupo / pixelio.de

More available books at **www.hansebooks.com**

THE SAVIOUR'S BIBLE.

A DIVINE REVELATION.

BY PHILIP A. MARQUAM.

Marquam, Oregon,
A. D 1899.

Period First.

The Existence and Nature of God and the Creation of the Planetary System During a Period of About One and One-Third Million Years, Beginning at the Creation of the Universe and Ending at the Creation of Mankind on the Earth.

1. God is a fluid substance and has life and intelligence. Its existence is eternal and without cause. It is the supreme power, Before any universe was formed. It was the only substance, power and intelligence that did exist, and It inhabited all space. It has power of thought, management and power to move and control Its substance. It has power to control the mind of mankind and reveal facts that have existed or taken place prior to mankind's existence, and some things that will take place in the future. It created the universe.

2. God created the planets by collecting a portion of Its substance in body forms and forced, or caused, the center of the bodies to revolve or turn around at a rapid rate, which naturally created friction, electricity and heat. The heat melted the substance of the bodies into a lava form the outside surroundings of the bodies was much cooler than the bodies, which, in course of time, caused the outside of the bodies to become solid and harden. The outside of the bodies, becoming solid, confined the heat on the inside to an extent that it caused the heat to explode and in places forced its way through the solid portion of the bodies. The heat in the bodies continued to explode and in places forced lava through the outside shell of the bodies in large quantities. A vapor that naturally passed off from the heat of the explosions, in course of time changed into a water and an atmosphere. The water covered, or extended, around the entire bodies, which petrified the outside of the bodies. The water

gradually became less by evaporation from the heat of the sun and from the heat of the explosions, and it finally failed to cover the entire bodies. The lava that was forced out through the outside shell of the bodies in large quantities, becoming petrified, is what principally formed the hills and mountains. The portions that the water failed to cover formed the principal part of the land. When the explosions took place they left openings in places through the outside shell of the bodies. The openings formed some of the openings of the volcanoes. The heat and fire that is forced out of the openings of some volcanoes comes from the heat and lava that is in the center of the bodies. A vapor that passed off from the heat of the volcanoes feeds the atmosphere, which prevents it from losing its present formation. The planets and secondary planets were created for the purpose of being inhabited by beings similar to that of the earth.

3. The other planets are inhabited by beings similar to mankind of the earth, and are the size and form of the inhabitants of the earth, and use written language. Some of the inhabitants of the other planets are only beginning to become civilized and some are farther advanced in civilization than the inhabitants of the earth. The suns were formed similar to the planets. Our solar system was formed for the benefit of the inhabitants of the solar planets. The sun's revolution causes its electricity to be in a traveling or revolving motion, which draws the solar planets around it.

4. The earth is hollow. The heat on the inside is continually in motion, is the cause of its daily revolution. The heat being in a revolving motion, causes its electricity to be in a revolving motion, which draws everything on the earth towards its center. The atmosphere is held to the earth by the electricity. The electricity of the earth, being in a revolving motion, draws the moon around it. The earth was 1,092,052 years old from the time it first began to form, up to the first creation of mankind.

5. The entire planetary system is formed in such a way

that the planets will be inhabited by mankind on an average of about 5,000,000 years. The planets, on an average, were about one and one-third million years old up to the time mankind was first born on the earth. Planetary systems have been formed for countless ages, and the planets were inhabited by mankind and have served their time in space and have passed back to their original substance. Some of the present comets are suns and planets that have existed prior to the present planetary system. The suns and planets that are now comets have at one time bursted, or the heat on the inside have exploded, and forced an opening out through one side, which causes a blaze of fire to pass off from the heat. The blaze forms the tail of comets.

Period Second.

The Creation, Birthplace and Primitive Existence of Mankind, and the Creation of Intelligent Beings and Vegetation of the Earth During a Period of Ten Thousand Years, Beginning with the Creation of Mankind and Ending on the 23rd Day of March, 1898, A. D., Which Would be the Expiration of Ten Thousand Years of Mankind's Existence on Earth. This Period Should be Considered the Dark Ages.

1. The way mankind was created, God took a portion of Its substance through a certain process in such a way that it formed a collection of matter in bodies which we might consider in the form of eggs, and as the eggs of matter were formed, God created the germs of mankind in the eggs out of a portion of Its substance, life and Its intelligence. The intelligence, while in the germs, was in a dormant, or unconscious existence. The temperature and surroundings of the eggs caused the germs to develop, both in size and intellect, and in about nine months from the time the germs were created, the birth took place in an infant form.

2. God directly fed mankind while in an infant form and until they grew to full size and partly developed in language, although to some extent mankind has had to depend on their own effort for support. When first placed on earth, mankind was a hairy being and remained so for thousands of years, living similar to animals, and in this primitive existence they lived hundreds of years. The existence of mankind is eternal; they have existed prior to their present existence; they are unconscious of their past existence; are an independent being; or a free agent, and are at liberty to act or refuse to act. When death takes place, the intelligence of mankind dwells on another shore for a period of time in another body, and we are still in a progressive state of existence. Our future state of existence will be more fully explained later on.

3. There are ten different races of mankind on the earth, and were on the earth at different periods and places. The first race of mankind, 633 in number, was born in India, Asia, on the 24th day of March, and soon after, in the year of 1. The year of one is ten thousand years prior to 1898, A.D. The Jewish race principally sprung from the first race. Dates of time should begin at the birth of the first race of mankind. The 23rd day of March, 1898, A. D., would be the expiration of ten thousand years beginning at the birth of the first race of mankind, which would be the year of 1. The year of 1 should begin at the expiration of every ten thousand years. The second year of 1 should begin on the 24th day of March, 1898, A. D., making the 24th day of March, A. D., the first day of the second year of 1. The second race of mankind, 209 in number, was born in Asia in the year 805. The Arabians principally sprung from the second race. In the year 813 there were 997 born, in the year 910 there were 705 born, and in the year 1003 there were 407 born, all in Asia. The three races are what the Chinese, Japanese and Russians princiaplly sprung from. In the year 1851 there were 1303 born in Europe. These are what the English, Irish, Scotch, Scandinavians and Germans principally sprung from. In the year 1910 there were 1102 born in Europe. These are what the French and Spanish principally sprung from. In the year 6075 there were 73 born in Africa. In the year 7018 there were 51 born in South America. In the year 7033 there were 107 born in North America. The three races are what the Indians and Negroes sprung from.

4. Mankind became so barbarous and domineering in the way of ruling in their primitive existence, that in the year 4732 God inflicted them with a disease which shortened their days. This disease was principally the cause of them losing their hair on their bodies. They were inflicted with this disease that they might be held in check and thus assist the civilization of mankind. The disease is the result of living beings which are continually eating at the bodies of mankind-and dying in the flesh and blood. The above men-

tioned beings should be called unseen germs. When I speak of unseen germs I do not mean the common microbe. The unseen germs are so small that mankind has failed to fully discover them. They exist in water and to some extent in vegetation, such as vegetables and fruit. Each drop of water on land and sea contains about 5000 unseen germs. These unseen germs are so light that to some extent they ascend with the vapor and return to the earth in the raindrops. They can live for weeks on a dry board without any food or water. It is the nature of them, when they come in contact with the flesh of mankind, to continually eat the flesh and suck the blood. They work on every organ of the body, including the blood and brain, which causes disease and insanity. The unseen germ enters the body of mankind when water and food are taken. When the unseen germ enters the stomach of mankind a portion of them are soon forced out into the flesh or system, and live in that condition for a time, and eventually die. Their bodies decay and pass out of the system in the way of pimples, boils, carbuncles and otherwise. There are about 3,000,000,000 dead unseen germs that pass out of the system in the corruption of a large carbuncle. A man that is of a small frame and weighs about 200 pounds carries around with him about 30,000,000,000 dead and alive bodies of unseen germs, and a man that is of a medium frame and weighs 300 pounds carries about 160,000,000,000. We might consider a man of that kind a graveyard for dead germs. The cause of a cancer is the unseen germs forming into a body and then eating the flesh as they travel. Sometimes the body breaks off in separate pieces, which is what forms what is called the roots of a cancer. During this period God indirectly revealed principles to mankind in the way of progression or developing in to civilization. The heathen bibles are not divine revelations. But they establish the fact that God was working on the minds of the people in those days. Some of the statements in the heathen bibles are true, but to take them as a whole they wonderfully misrepresent matters. The old Jewish bible in its early age was intended by the writers as a law of God. That is the man God that they worshiped in those days. The Jewish religion became so powerful that God sent a Saviour into the world to partly break down the Jewish religion and to raise mankind to a higher degree of civilization. The Saviour was born on Mount Tabor, in Gallilee, in the year 7973. His mother was the wife of a man by the name of Nazaree, and his given name was Jesus. So he went by the name of Jesus Nazaree. He grew in divine wisdom from a child and began at the age of 17 years to teach the people the proper principles and opposing the Jewish religion. He had many followers and great multitudes of people attended his lectures. He had no power to forgive sin and did not claim that He did. His divine knowledge was far superior to the average man. .At many times during his lectures divine power and blessings fell upon the people. Those of the Pharisee kind, learning that He rejected the Jewish religion tried many ways to put him to death, and finally organized into what we might consider a mob and disguised themselves and led the Saviour away awhile before day in the morning of the 3d day of May, in the year 8000, and shamefully crucified Him. The Christian bible, called the New Testament, contains principally priestcraft, although it makes a number of statements that are true in regard to the Saviour's teachings. Soon after the Saviour's departure the priests began to write what we might call transcripts, using some of the Saviour's words, and in places wonderfully misrepresenting his language. There were twenty-three men crucified after the Saviour's departure all represented by the priests as being the Saviours of the world. In the year 8291 the followers of one of these above mentioned Saviours called Christ overpowered, the rest and organized into one branch and completed the Christian bible called the New Testament, and destroyed the other transcripts. This branch, later on developed into the Catholic church, and later on it split, and Luther organized the

Protestant church. The whole of the Christian churches principally grew from the Saviour's teaching. Christ's day was not until about one hundred years after the true Saviour's death. The writers of the New Testament give Christ the name of Jesus, which we might consider was stole from the true Saviour. Christ was only a priest and had no power to forgive sins or perform miracles. The statements in the the Christian bibles concerning Christ performing miracles was written after Christ was dead, some, almost two hundred years after. The Mohammedon bible teachings are absurd and deceptive.

5. All intelligent beings are created similar to that of mankind. Some of the intelligent beings of water and land were created for the purpose of mankind in the way of food. Some of the wild animals and such things as flies, fleas, lice, bugs, jackets and many other things similar to those above mentioned, were created for the purpose of assisting the civlization of mankind. Some of the vegetation was created for the benefit of mankind in the way of food. Such things as weeds, fern, lambquarter, cockeral, wild oats, tobacco, tea, coffee, opium, etc., were also principally created for the purpose of advancing the civilization of mankind. God created the vegetation by first creating the germs in the soil. The germs were created out of a portion of its life and substance and were placed in the soil where It desired them to grow, while the temperature and surroundings caused the germs to develop and grow into whatever plant or tree for which they were intended.

Period Third.

The Proper Form of Government and the Probability of a Grand Advancement of Civilization During a Period of a Thousand Years, Beginning on the 24th Day of March, 1898 A. D., Which Would be the First Day of the Second Year of I, and Ending at the Expiration of One Thousand Years.

1. This period is God's day on earth. Not that God has power to dwell on earth in the form of man, but It is to deal more direct and be in nearer relation with mankind than It has ever before. It is to reveal all necessary facts to mankind. How the world should be conducted or managed. A Saviour of man is to dwell one thousand years on earth during this period to conduct this great day of God's in the way of completing civilization. The Saviour of man has made Its appearance in an unexpected way. He has been born the second time, that is his mind or intelligence has been born a second time. His mind that dwells in his present body once dwelt in his body that was born on Mt. Tabor, in Gallilee. He has two earthly mothers but no earthly father. It is a mystery to mankind and always will be how the mind of a man can be born a second time; but it is not so much more of a mystry than the plan of the creation of mankind as explained in period second. He should be recognized by his parent name as far as citizenship is concerned or in the way of transacting any business. He has to depend on his own efforts for support, and is subject to all difficulties of life. He has no power to forgive sins or to perform miracles, but his knowledge is far superior to that of mankind in a divine sense. In one sense He is the Saviour of this world—to save mankind from degenerating and to save the world from going to destrction, as described in Period Fourth, and to save mankind from becoming diseased and dying in early life. His mission on earth is to teach mankind how life can be prolonged, and to

instruct mankind during this period to be ready to begin the building of Paradise at the beginning of the Period Fourth. God has kept back the knowledge from mankind in regard to the disease that causes short life until this day, so when mankind learns that life can be prolonged to an extent that they can live hundreds of years at the present age of the world, then they will believe that this period is what it is represented to be, and this book is a divine revelation. The coming of this day has been named the Millenium, so I will let it remain so.

2. There should be only one government on each continent and each government should be an independant republic. The republic should be divided into states. The states should be laid off as nearly as convenient with the geographical lay of the country and should be as large as practicable. The seat of government on each continent should be near the center of the continent. The official members of each government should pricipally consist of president, house of representatives, and all necessary officers. The president should be elected by a majority of the legal voters of the nation. Representatives should be elected by a majority of the legal voters of the states. There should be one representative to every one hundred thousand legal voters in the. state. Each government should publish a newspaper, and any political principle at issue among the people should be published in the national papers at least three months prior to the general election, except in case of necessity. All principles that the people desire to become a law, the representatives should form in bills and vote on the bills, and it should require a majority of the votes of the representatives to pass the bills. The presidents should have no veto power, and it should be their duty to sign all bills passed by the representatives. The elections should be held once a year, and the house of representatives should be held in session long enough to dispose of all bills that were published in the national papers. It should be the duty of the representatives

to pass laws according to the wish of the people as near as can be ascertained.

3. The states should have no power to pass laws except through their representatives at the seat of the national government. The seat of each state should be near the center and its official members should consist principally of governor, secretary, treasurer, and other necessary officers, and their duty should be to enforce or carry out the national laws and to manage and control the public works as provided by law. Each state should publish a paper for the benefit of the legal voters.

The Millennium Banner should be twenty inches by about twenty-nine and made of solid red, with a block of blue in the center on both sides ten inches square. Five white stars should be in a circle on the block of blue. The Word "Millennium" should be printed in large white letters above the block of blue, and the word "Banner" below. It should be edged with golden braid on the sides and top and golden fringe on the bottom and a golden tassel on each lower corner. The five stars and printed letters should be on both sides. The five stars represent the principle of the five continents developing into five independent republics.

The Millenium badge should be made on the same plan as the Millenium banner, except in size it should be about one and one-half inches wide and two and one-half- inches long.

4. The government should own and control all of the land and mines on their respective continents and adjoining islands, should manufacture all goods, implements, machinery, building of boats, and should own and control all railroads, public highways, telegraph, telephone, and electric lights, and should build cities, residences, carry on public business in the way of selling good, or whatever nature it might be. The lands should be divided into 40 acres lots, and the lots should be divided into townships. Townships should be 24 lots each way, and should be in rows in a line with the general survey of the continent as near as practicable. There

should be a 40 foot space between the townships, and a 60 foot space in the center of each township leading north and south and east and west. The 60 foot spaces divide the township into quarters. A quarter should be a block.. The lots should be in double rows leading north and south in the block. A double row containing 24 lots should be called a row. A 40 foot space should be between each of the rows north and south, except in the center of the township. The 60 fot spaces leading north and south and east and west should answer the purpose. Two car tracks should lead through the center of each township, north and south and east and west, on a plan so that both steam and electric cars could run on them. Two electric car tracks should lead through the forty fot space leading north and south and east and west between the townships. Two electric car tracks should lead through the 40 feet space between the rows leading north and south in the blocks. There should be a turn table at each end of the car line between the rows in connection with the car lines leading east and west between the townships. In places where there are rocks and hills they should be removed to the low waste lands. There should be a two story residence on each lot on the side joining the electric car tracks. The residences should be twenty-four by twenty-four feet. It should be on a plan so that it could be well ventilated. Each lot should be fenced with an iron fence.

5. There should be a city in the center of the township. Twenty acres of land should be reserved for that purpose. There should be a space of forty feet around the city. The sixty foot spaces that lie through the townships should be streets in the cities. There should be a sidewalk ten feet wide leading north and south and east and west through the city, one on each side of the street. The streets divide the city into quarters. There should be a general merchandise store on the north-west corner of the southeast quarter large enough to supply the citizens of the entire township. As near

as convenient, goods should be put up in boxes, kegs, buckets, packages, sacks, bottles, and not kept for sale in bulk in a way that they would have to be measured or weighed when sold. except when absolutely necessary. There should be a five story building a hundred and sixty by a hundred and sixty feet in the center of the said southeast quarter, to be used as schools and colleges. There should be a hotel on the northeast corner of the southeast quarter, used principally for the government employes. There should be a two story chapel a hundred and sixty by a hundred and sixty feet in the center of said southwest quarter. It should be arranged with steeple and bell. The grounds of the chapel should be arranged with walks, flowers and ornamental trees. There should be a building on the southeast corner of the northwest quarter arranged for the purpose of holding courts and elections in, and with offices for all the township officials, such as justice, constable, township attorney, city marshal, school superintendent, dentist, physician, or any other necessary officer, including the daily press and township jail. And there should be a building in the center of said northwest quarter for the purpose of manufacturing electricity for the entire township. When water power can be had it is advisable to use it in the manufacture of electricity. There should be a crematory and healing institute on the north side of the said northwest quarter. On the southwest corner of the northeast quarter there should be a building for the purpose of all necesasry shops, such as blacksmith, shoe, tin, harness, barber, butcher, wood repair, iron repair, jewelry, baker, tailor, milliner and dressmaking shops, also ice factory. In the center of said northeast quarter there should be a flouring and all necessary mills. On the east side of the northeast quarter there should be a feed stable, slaughter house and all necessary buildings for the purpose of keeping stock. On the west side of the said quarter there should be a building and grounds for the purpose of holding fairs and expositions. There should be lots fifty by a hundred feet joining on the sidewalk north and south and east and west; these lots should be called city lots; and there should be a family residence twenty-four by twenty-four feet on the end of each city lot joining the sidewalks. There should be a four story building sixty by sixty feet in the center of the city direct on the street crossing. The lower floor to be used for a stroage room, and should be on a plan that cars could pass through each way. The second floor to be for telephone, telegraph and distributing postoffice. The third floor to be on a plan of a fort and used for convenience of necessary home guards. There should be a furnace on the fourth floor for the purpose of boiling and preparing water for the use of citizens of the township. This building should be called the depot. A large clock should be on the top of this building, facing the four sides. There should be a flagstaff extending from the top of this building with a golden ball on the top of the staff. The flag of the nation should be imitated by the millenium banner, with the name of the continent printed on the flag. A cistern should be directly under the depot forty by forty feet, and be not less than two hundred feet deep, and when necessary should be as much as five hundred feet deep. It should be walled up twenty feet with stone, and walls should be every few feet apart twenty feet high, and the top of the walls to be covered with stone. A water pipe should lead from the bittom of the cistern to the fourth floor of the depot, and the space above the walls should be filled up and the top should be on a plan so that surface water coud not seep through.

6. Iron posts shoud be set leading from the depot on each side of the 60 foot space leading through the township, and on each side of the 40 foot space between the rows, also on each side of the space between the townships leading north and south. Electric lights and telephone wires should lead from the second floor of the depot, supported on posts, to every residence and business house in the township. Telphone and telegraph wires should lead from the second floor

PERIOD THIRD.   17

of the depot to a second floor of the adjoining depot. A double stone wall should lead from the depot on each side of the 60 foot space through the township and on each side of the 40 foot space. The walls should be about four foot apart and about six feet high, with a stone bottom and a top made water tight, and set underground. It should be used for water pipe leading from the fourth floor of the depot sufficient to supply the entire township with water. aily cars should run from the depot to all parts of the township for the benefit of passengers and for the purpose of delivering and receiving mail and supplies for the people of the township. There should be two sets of employes to run the cars. One set should begin at four o'clock a. m. and run until 12 m., and the other set should begin at 12 m. and run until 8 p. m. The buildings of the township should all be made of stone, and on a plan so they could be taken down and removed. No one should be allowed to live in the city under the age of thirty years or to hold any offices.

7. The justice should be the leading officer of the township and all lawsuits of the township should be brought before him, or her, as the case may be, and in some cases a jury should be allowed. Every person should be allowed a fair and impartial trial; the evidence and proceedings of the court shoull be in writing, and persons losing cases of importance should have a right to take the same to the supreme court, which should be at the seat of the state. Any one convicted of crime of importance should be compelled to serve on public works at the rate of eight hours per day, and not be confined only at night time and when necessary.

8. There should be but one rule for weights. Three hundred and fifty grains should make one ounce and twenty ounces, or 7000 grains, should make one pound. The government should place gold and silver on deposit, and as near as convenient it should be in blocks. One ounce, or 350 grains of gold, should be 20 dollars, and one ounce, or 350 grains of silver, should be one dollar. Paper bills should be

issued to represent the gold and silver on deposit. There should be issued a twenty dollar bill to represent one ounce of gold on deposit. They should be a legal tender for all debts of twenty dollars or more, except when small change is required. Gold bills should not be issued in any denomination except in twenty dollar bills. Ten dollar bills shoud be issued to represent ten ounces of silver. They should be a legal tender for all debts of one hundred dollars or less, except when small change should be required. There should be issued five dollar bills to represent five ounces of silver. They should be legal tender for all debts of fifty dollars or less, except when small change is required. There should be issued one dollar bills to represent one ounce of silver. They should be a legal tender for all debts of ten doll ars or less, except when small change is also required. Silver bills should not be issued in any other denomination except as above described. The minor coins should be about 95 per cent. copper and about 5 per cent. tin and zinc. The weight of fifty cents should be 210 grains. The weight of twenty-five cents should be 170 grains. The weight of ten cents should be 90 grains. The weight of one cent should be 50 grains. There should be large figures on each side of the minor coins according to the denomination thereof, and the name of the continent around the border. Minor coins should be a legal tender for all debts of 99 cents or less and when required for change. Gold or silver ore or coin should not be a legal tender for any debts, and when any one desires to move to some other country they should have a right to draw silver and gold on deposit to the amount of what paper bills they have in possession. Paper bills should be called in when they have been in circulation 20 years, and others issued in their stead, except those that prove to be lost, and the gold and silver that is on deposit that represent the bills that may be lost, should go to the general government.

9. There should be a law requiring each white male person to pass an examination before the township's school su-

perintendent, and if his qualifications are sufficient he should have a right of franchise at the age of thirty years. The law should also require each white female person to pass an examination, and if her qualifications are sufficient, she should have a right of franchise at the age of fifty years. No person should have the right to marry under the age of twenty years. Marriage should be by a period of five years, and if the persons engaged in marriage live together agreeably at the expiration of five years, they should have a right to remarry, and on the same conditions at the expiration of every five years. When parties desire to marry, if they own property they should enter into a property contract in the way of dividing property before marriage, and the contract should be delivered to the justice and placed on file. At the expiration of each five years, if the parties who engage in marriage fail to live together agreeably, the justice should be notified of the fact by either party or any one concerned, and the contract should be placed on record and become valid. No unhealthy female under the age of fifty, or that is of the Negro or Indian races, should be allowed to marry. No unhealthy male person should be allowed to marry any woman that is under the age of fifty years. A male person that is of the Negro or Indian race should not be allowed to marry any woman under the age of fifty. No white female person under the age of fifty that is considered a noted thief or is not of a virtuous character should be allowed to marry. No white male person that is considered a noted thief or is not of a virtuous character should be allowed to marry any woman under the age of fifty. When a child is born, its name should be given to the justice with the name of its parents, and this should be placed on record. When parties desire to marry, their names should be given to the justice, and the place of birth, and it should be the duty of the jucstice to search the records and if the records show that the parties desiring to marry are not entitled to marry under the law proposed above, the marriage should be rejected. The township superintendent should be the proper person to perform the marriage ceremony. The Negro and Indian races should be prevented from increasing except a very few, which should be kept on some suitable island, and only enough of them should be allowed to marry to keep the races in existence. The Negroes and Indians were created more as a savage race than the white races were, and were placed on earth principally for the purpose of advancing the civilization of the white races. It is not Gol's design for the Negro or Indian races to mingle with the white races by marriage or otherwise. If these races were allowed at all times hereafter to mingle in marriage, the offspring would degenerate in about one-half million years to an extent that civilization would cease and mankind would not be much superior to the animals. The Negro and Indian races should not have the right of franchise or to hold office. It is God's design for the first seven races of mankind, being the white races, to mingle in marriage, become civilized, and be the controlling inhabitants of the earth. Women over the age of thirty and under the age of fifty, married or single, that have no children, should have a right to hold any office, clerk in stores, teach in schools, or carry on any business under government control, and hold all other positions of whatever kind and nature except that of president and representatives, which rule shall also apply to men. Women or men over the age of fifty should have the right to serve as president or representative. Under the present circumstances, the American mode of dress is about sufficient, but as civilization advances to an extent that mankind begin to retain the hair on their bodies, less and lighter quantity of clothing should be worn. There should be a company of fifty home guards in each township, and it should be their duty to meet at the fort to perform any duty when called upon by the justice. There should be one language only and that should be the English language, subject to some improvements. There should be a name for everything, and when one word represents two things, a new word should be added, e. g., sea and see. When the earth begins to be overpopulated, the government should provide means to check the increase of mankind according to the population. When any one is taken sick, they should be taken to the township healing institute and placed in the hands of the physician. When the world develops to five independent republics, reciprocity should be the proper way to regulate the tariff on goods as near as can be ascertained. The dead should be cremated at the township crematory. When a death takes place, as soon as convenient the proprietor of the telephone office should notify the people of the entire township in fact, stating who is dead and when the funeral will take place. The deceased should be taken to the chapel by the management of the township superintendent, and when the time arrives for the funeral to take place, the superintendent should deliver a brief oration at the chapel, a song to suit the occasion should be sung, and then order the pall bearers to start with the casket to the grounds of the creamatory. The superintendent should join the procession next carying the millenium banner. (On these accasions the millenium banner should be edged with black on the top and sides. The bottom should be edged with black fringe. The tassels should also be in black.) Each person in the procesion should have a millenium badge on their breast. On these occasions the millenium badge should be black, excepting the five stars on the face, which should be white. The near relation of the deceased should join the procesison next. Next, all the congregation. The procesion should march two abreast, and as the procesion starts to leave the grounds of the chapel, a black flag should be raised on top of the depot building and the bell of the chapel should be rung slowly during the march of the procesiosn. The casket should be placed on the crematory grounds and the relations and near friends of the deceased be allowed to gather around it for about fifteen minutes. Then the superintendent should deliver the casket to the proprietor of the crematory and dismiss the congregation, then order the black flag to be lowered. During the march of the procession the business houses should be closed. The cremation should take place one hour after the black flag is lowered. When a funeral of a state official takes place, there should be a black flag raised on top of depot building in each township within the state during the time the funeral services are supposed to take place; and when any national official dies, a black flag should be raised on top of each depot building within the nation or continent. The black flag to represent the funeral of a state official should be a little larger than the township funeral flag, and the flag that represents the funeral of a national official should be a little larger than the state funeral flag. When a national official dies, a black flag should be raised at the seat of government of all other nations at the time the funeral is supposed to take place.

10. A day should be one revolution of the earth. A week should be eleven days. The first ten days of the week should reypresent the first ten thousand years of mankind's existence on the earth, and the last day of the week should represent the millenium. A month should be three weeks, or 33 days. There should be eleven months in a year. A year should be one revolution of the earth around the sun. There would be eleven month and about two days in a year. The extra days should not be includede in the weeks or months, and the first one of thementioned days should be used as a general election day. There should be a name for each day in the week. The last day of the week should be called Sunday. There should be a name for each month.

11. There should be a township superintendent, and songs should be composed based on civilization. It should be the duty of the superintendent to hold religious services in the upper story of the chapel in the forenoon on Sunday. The services should be for the purposes of honoring God by delivering lectures on theology, science and mortality, and by giving God praise and thanks for our existence and for

what benefits we have received. On certain occasions honor should be given to those in authority over the nation. Songs should be sung in connection with instrumental music during services. The attendance should consist principally of those twenty years of age and older, and at the same time Sunday schools should be held on the first floor for thepurpose of teaching those under twenty years of age and over nine the principles of civilization. The afternoon of Sunday should be a time of recreation. The people of the township should engage in any kind of respectable amusements, such as car riding, wheeling, games of different kinds, picnic entertainments, socials, visiting, attending theatres and shows. It is advisable for any unmarried people to engage in dancing. I do not recommend that married people engage in dancing to any great extent. During the afternoon male or female should have a right to indulge in drinks of various kinds, with the exception of intoxicating liquors, which should be restricted to small quantities, and that that is drank should be of a mild proof. They also should have a right to partake of nuts, melons, fruits, or anything of that nature. All public business, or gatherings, or work of whatever nature it might be, excepting in case of necessity, should be performed or transacted in the day time, and not earlier than four o'clock a. m. nor later than nine o'clock p. m. All people should sleep from eight to twelve hours during the night time, as near as convenient. The chapels should be generally used for the purpose of holding all kinds of meetings and gatherings, except on Sunday forenoon, which time should always be set aside for religious services.

12. Those who reside in the United States and believe in the principles of civilization as their religious views, should unite by forming classes, and as soon as convenient should incorporate and carry out the principles as laid down in this book as near as can be done without infringing on the national and state laws of the United States. Each company should be an independent body, and its members should be

law abiding citizens, and when laws are not agreeable to their belief they should insist on having laws repealed by taking a legal process of law, and new laws should be made according to their belief. Companies should form their own rules and regulations according to the laws of their respective states. They should buy land in the companies' name and form townships and carry on whatever business they see fit. The banners of the companies should be the millenium banner. The first day of the present weeks, called Sunday, should be used by the members of the companies to hold religious services, before laws can be repealed, and any one that believes in those principles and does not belong to the above described companies or classes should not be duty bound to observe the day called Sunday, except in the way of observing the state and national laws of the United States. Those that believe in those principles as described in this book should consider them sacred and not abuse them. There should be a law to punish any one who willfully speaks abusive of those principles. They should be sent to the Island to live with the Negro and Indian races, never to return. The Companies should send qualified teachers to different parts of the United States with instructions to teach the principles of civilization and organize classes. This book should be sent to different nations, and when different nations adopt those principles treaties should be made between nations favoring the principles laid down in this book. Those that accept this book as divine revelation should favor laws giving the government a right to loan money at a low rate of interest, secured by real estate, to buy land, manufacture goods, build railroads, and carry on business of different kinds, as soon as means affords. This should be kept up until the governments own and control the land of the world. No government should take land from the owner by force of armies. The American flag should be retained as an emblem of the nation until it is set aside by a legal process of law enacted by the American people. Any nation that develops to an independent republic should use the millenium banner as the flag of their nation, with the name of their country printed thereon instead of the words millenium banner. And the five stars should be in the upper corner of the flag next to the staff.

Period Fourth.

A Proper Form of Single Government, and Removing the Continents to the Equator. The Building of Paradise, During a Period of Nine Thousand Years, Beginning at the Expiration of Period Third and Ending at the Expiration of Nine Thousand Years.

1. In this period all governments should become one. There should be only one president for the world and other necessary officers to carry on the business of the government. The government should be a pure democracy. The election should be held once a year at the time described in period third. There should be a national newspaper issued by the general government and each legal voter should be entitled to one. When political principles are at issue, it should be published in bill form in the national paper not less than six months prior to the election excepting in case of necessity. All legal voters should be at liberty to vote for or against the bill. No person under the age of fifty years, or one who is afflicted with old age or feebleness, should have the right of franchise, and no one under the age of thirty years should have the right to live in the city. The national flag should be solid red with a block of blue in the center, and with a large white star in the center of the block representing the nation.

2. Each continent and most all islands should be moved to the equator. The government should begin the work in Africa or South America and empty the rock on the equator between the two continents. The rock, before being used, should be crushed reasonably fine. Railroads should be built for the purpose of removing the rock and land. About forty thousand revolving turn tables should be constructed at the end of the railroads where the rock should be unloaded, for the purpose of unloading the rock. The soil and clay and all

valuables on the equator and a reasonable distance from the equator on South America or Africa should be removed to the outer portions of the continent, and the rock and gravel along the equator should be worked down almost on a level of the sea. Then the soil and clay of the same continent should be removed to the equator of the same continent and the outer portion of the same continent should be worked down to the bottom of the sea. Except a portion should be left for railroad to be built on, leading to the other continents. When South America and Africa are thus worked down one of the other continents at a time should be worked down to the sea and some places it would be safe to go below the bottom of the sea. All continents and most of the islands should thus be worked down within a certain distance of the equator, and as the rock foundation which has been built on the equator becomes solid, the clay and soil is to be placed thereon. The rock and land at the equator should be made as wide as the material will make it. The gold, silver and precious stones, perifactions and fossils, or any curiosities found in the earth, should be preserved for future use. Small volcanoes should be filled up and large, active ones be left alone. A sufficient number of islands should be left and enough of all kinds of animals or any living creature of the animal kind should be kept on those islands to an extent to keep them in existence. When the entire work of removing the land to the equator has been completed, it should be called the belt of the earth. The north edge of the belt should be a little further north of the equator than the south edge should be south of the equator. The water of the earth should be boiled and bottled and the sides of the belt should be walled with stone. The filth and anything of value should be moved from the bottom of sea. Then when all of the germs that cause disease are destroyed the water should be so boiled and emptied.

3. Paradise should be made on the belt. It should be in five departments. The first department to be on the north

sideof the belt around the earth east and west laid off in townshipssimilar to those described in Period Third, and should be for those under the age of fifty to reside in. No one under the age of thirty should have a right to live in the city. The second department should join the first on the south, extending around the earth east and west, and should also be laid off in townships similar to those described in Period Third. It should be in a line leading north and south with the townships in department first, and should be only for those from the age of fifty to eleven hundred years to reside in. The third department should be directly in the center of the belt leading north and south around the earth, and should be twenty-four miles wide, and there should be a stone wall on each side of the third department extending around the earth east and west. There should be a river in the center of this department east and west around the earth, one hundred feet wide and two hundred and fifty feet deep the bottom and sides should be walled with stone, and the side walls and bottom should be made double, with a four inch space between; the four inch space should be filled with cement, and the entire walls should be made water tight. A small cistern should be about every one mile apart under the bottom wall. The cisterns should be walled with stone. Pipes should lead from the cisterns near the top of the walls for the purpose of supplying the river with water. The pipes should be on a plan so that the mouth of them could be closed to prevent the water from running in at all times. When necessary the pipes should be closed up and the walls cleaned. The river should be for the purpose of boat riding around the earth. It should not be kept full of water, so the boats could pass under the car tracks leading north and south. A bridge should extend around the earth direct over the river, 100 feet high, with five floors. The upper floor should be with sides and made water tight and used for the purpose of sailing around the earth in small sail boats, and the other floors should be for the purpose of car and wheel riding around the earth.

PERIOD FOURTH. 29

The sides of each floor should be covered with wire screen work, and there should be elevators at every north and south railroad along the bridge.

There should be a hotel about every one hundred miles around the earth next to the river for the accommodation of those traveling around the earth. Electric car tracks should lead north and south through this department in a line with the north and south car lines leading north and south in the other department. The townships in this department should include the land between the outer walls and the river and between the north and south car lines in this department that is on a line with the north and south car lines between the townships in the other departments. The north and south car lines in this department that are on a line with the north and south car lines in and near the center of the townships in the other departments divide the township into halves. Each half should be a block. There would be two blocks in a township in this third department. A lot in this department should be forty feet and should lead east and west through the blocks. A space of ten feet should be between every other lot leading east and west. The lots between the space should be called a row, and there would be 802 lots in a row. Electric car tracks should lead east and west through the ten foot space between the rows. There should be a one story residence on each lot, twenty-four by twenty-four feet, the walls of which should be made with open bars similar to those of a cage. There should be a depot on each side of the river on all car lines leading north and south that are on a range with the car lines in the center of the townships in the other departments. The depot should be about six miles from the outer walls of this department and made on a plan described in Period Third. Water pipes, electric lamps and telephone lines should lead from the depots to every residence in the township and a telephone and telegraph wire should lead to the other depots in this department and to depots in the other departments. There should be a beautiful grove surrounding the depots in this third department, which groves should be arranged with seats, grand stands and all necessary provisions. Precious stones and petrifications of sea and land or any curiosities found in the earth should be kept in these groves. They should also be arranged with fountains, flowers, and ornamental trees. Religious services, entertainments, etc., should be held in these groves. None but those from one hundred to eleven hundred years of age, and who are cleansed from all disease, are of good reputation and have a good moral character should be allowed to reside in this department, and this department is not intended for those who reside therein to perform any labor excepting the necessary work at their residences. It is intended as a place of pleasure in the way of wheeling and boat and car riding around the earth.

4. The fourth department should be south of the third department around the earth, and should be divided into townships similar to those described in Period Third, and should be in a line with the townships north and south leading through the other departments. This department should be for those of eleven hundred years old and until they become almost helpless. The citizens of this department should have no right of franchise.

5. The fifth department should be south of the fourth department around the earth, and should be arranged principally with suitable buildings for the aged to live in after they have served their time in the fourth department. They should remain in this department till death. This department should be arranged with proper crematories for the purpose of disposing of the dead. The car lines leading north and south should be on a line with the car lines in the other departments. The five departments should be called Paradise.

6. The space leading north and south through the departments in the center of the townships should be sixty feet wide at the outer sides of the belt. The earth, being round,

it would leave a wider space in the center of the belt. There should be one car track on each side of the above described space and one through the center. The land between the car tracks should be left vacant except the portion used for the cities, and groves as described in department third, and other necessary purposes. A portion of the vacant land should be planted in shade trees and used for wheel riding and other amusements. Car tracks should lead through the townships as described in Period Third, in department first, second and fourth, except in the above described space, and in department third. Underground tiling should lead from the outside of the belt within three hundred feet of the river through the part of the belt in Africa and South America, which is not necessary to remove below the level of the sea. The tiling should be of stone, and the inside opening should be about two by two feet and should be placed underground about fifty feet and about three hundred feet from the depots on the car lines leading north and south. The land should be lowered about twenty feet below the surface through the portion of Africa and South America and filled up with crushed rock or gravel or clay and soil placed thereon. Ten acres of land should be reserved on each lot in departments first, second and fourth, on the side adjoining the car tracks leading north and south, for building purposes and for an orchard, shrubbery, ornamental trees and gardens.

Ten acres of land should be used for timber culture in each lot. At the expiration of about every fifty years the timber should be grubbed and another ten acres planted. All waste timber should be sawed into saw dust, which should be spread on cultivated land, and also waste straw, manure and excrement in each department, and plowed under. There should be wind mills along the river in the third department situated where the north and south car tracks should cross the river. The wind mills should be so arranged that water could be pumped up into the water floor, about one hundred feet above the river. Pipes should lead from the water floor above the river, supported on posts about twenty feet high, to each residence building and all of the land in each department, on a plan that all Paradise could be sprinkled with water drawn from the river. The water used for drinking, bathing, washing and cooking purposes should be led from the depots. Cars should be run from the depots through all of the departments for the purpose of delivering and receiving mail and provisions. There should be a fence around the residences in each department, and a water closet at the front side of the yard of each residence, with a door on the side outside to open under the seat. Proper vessels should be kept under the seats, and the slops shipped daily and spread on cultivated lands. There should be no cesspools, sewers or underground cellars in either department. There should be a canal about two feet wide and four feet deep leading from the river on each side of the river, under the car tracks leading north and south through the center of the townships through each department. The canals should be walled in with stone and made water tight. Tiling should be placed underground about two and one-half feet leading from the canals east and west through the townships for drainage and irrigating purposes. The canals should be furnished with water from the river by wind mill force and should be on a plan so that the ends on the outer portion of the belt could be left open or closed up.

7. Each township block and lots should be numbered, and also each city lot, and mail or goods should be addressed as below described, e. g.:

> John Smith,
> Department First,
> Township 4,
> Block 3,
> Lot 1.

The continents should be moved to the equator by the expiration of this Period, for the reason that, under the present circumstances, the heat of the sun is gradually evaporating the water of the earth at the equator to an extent that the earth will be in a condition so mankind can not live thereon in a little over one million years. The government should collect a certain per cent. or profit on the different branches of the industry, except in the fifth department. In the third department the government should collect by the year from the inhabitants thereof. This collection should commence in Period Third and end at the expiration of mankind on the earth. The general government should keep a correct record of dates of time beginning at the year of ten thousand years prior to 1898 after Christ.

Period Fifth.

Mankind's Long and Happy Existence in Paradise and the Final End of Mankind and the Universe, During a Period of Over Four and One-half Million Years, Beginning at the expiration of Period Fourth and Ending at the Expiration of Mankind on Earth. This Period Should Begin on the Third Year of I.

1. No one in this period should be generally allowed to eat but one meal a day, as near as practicable in the morning. All rules of civilization should be observed to an extent that mankind will retain the hair on their bodies as they did in their primitive existence, and if all rules of civilization are strictly observed it will enable some to live sixteen or seventeen hundred years. No one in this period should have a right of franchise under the age of one hundred or over the age of eleven hundred years. Marriage in this period should be from one to five years, just as parties that desire to marry could agree on. The national flag should be solid red, with a block of blue in the center and a white star in the center of the blue block, to represent the nation, and five small stars should be in a circle around the center star to represent the five departments of Paradise. In this priod the years should be divided into weeks and months. Five days should be a week. The first four days should represent the first four periods as described in this book, and the last day of the week should represent the last period. Thirty days, or six weeks, should be a month, and there would be twelve months and about a week in a year. The extra week in the year should not be included in the month, but should be called the Annual Week. When political principles are at issue they should be published in a bill form in the national paper one year prior to the election, except in case of necessity, and the legal voters should vote directly on the bill. All general

elections should be held on the first day of the annual week and officers elected should take their positions on the last day of the annual week. On the day after the expiration of every ten thousand years should be a general holiday set apart as a day to give honors to God for the Saviour's day on earth. Beginning in the year twenty thousand, which would be on the third year of one services should be in groves in the form of lectures referring back to the Saviour's day, and in the way of songs, conducted similar to the way the Saviour's way of conducting his meetings while on earth. On the first day after the expiration of every million years should be a general holiday set apart as a day to give special honor to God. The people of the world should meet at the grove in department third and at the chapel ground in department first and second for that purpose.

2. This period is to be a time of happiness. Domestic torubles should cease to exist and wars should be no more. The sun is becoming more solid on its surafce, and in less than five million years its heat will not be sufficient to supply the vegetation and mankind of the earth. When the government find that mankind is beginning to perish for the need of the heat of the sun and the proper atmosphere, the increase of mankind should be prevented. The remainder of the universe will serve its proper time in space and eventally pass back to its original existence.

Treatment.

This Department is not Intended to be Read in Public, Except in the Way of References Made By Public Speakers when Lecturing on diseases.

No. 1—PROPER RULES.

The disease that causes short life should be treated as below described by those between the age of forty and fifty years and are in reasonable good health to begin with. It would be impossible to lay down a plan of treatment sufficient for parties of all ages and those that are afflicted with different diseases. Those of the above age, who desire to prolong life, should confine themselves as nearly as practicable to one meal a day, and that meal should be served in the morning, but to some extent eating should be regulated according to the labor to be performed. A person who is inclined to be fleshy and is not compelled to labor very hard, can do on one meal per day, and the lean person, who is not compelled to labor very hard, should eat the morning meal, and a mild lunch between the hours of twelve m. and five p. m. When hard labor is to be performed, either party should eat more according. Food should be seasoned with salt and cooked well done. As to the kind of food, beef, mutton, poultry and fish are the proper food in the way of meats, except when very hard labor is to be performed, then hog meat is proper food. I cannot advise the eating of hog meat for every day use. Wheat and corn flour are proper food for bread, coarse ground. Most all fruits and vegetables are proper food, and berries in case the seeds are separated. I can not advise too much eating of what are called nicnacs, such as sweet cake and preserves. Under the one meal system one can eat all he desires of the above mentioned food at the morning meal. Boiled water, when desired, with a little sugar and cream, is the proper table drink, and should be drunk hot. Too much eating in the afternoon does not give the stomach and bowels proper time to rest during the hours of sleep. The three meal system causes some to be too fleshy, and to some extent it causes rheumatism, headache, irregularity of the bowels, piles, dyspepsia, restless nights, and the falling of the womb, and insanity, and other diseases, and also short life. No one should ever try the one meal system unless they use the wholesome water according to the direction described in this book, for the reason when you begin to eat only one meal per day or one meal and a lunch, the unseen germs gnaw at some of the inward organs more extensively than they do when you eat three meals per day. But by drinking the wholesome water causes them to let loose of the organs and pass out. The necessity of cooking food done and boiling the water is to kill all germs. Those who desire to live long should live in a way so no living beings of any size, from a tapeworm to an unseen germ, could exist in their bodies. The idea advanced by some that mankind cannot live without living beings existing in their bodies, cannot be established as a fact, and is absolutely false.

No. 2—WHOLESOME WATER.

Have made to order jars about one foot in diameter and and about two feet high, with a faucet in the side, made of good material. The faucet should be six inches above the bottom of the jars. Have tin lids made for the jars with a rim around the outer edge sufficient to extend about two inches below the top of the jars on the outside. Place the faucet jars on a shelf fixed for that purpose, with the faucet extending over the edge of the shelf, and put one-half ounce of unslaked lime in the jars to each gallon of water that you intend to add. If the lime is air slaked, add a little more. There should be enough lime added to slightly flavor the water. Boil the water, and let it boil three or four minutes after it comes to a boil, then pour the boiling water while hot into the jars and put the lids on the jars. Let it set three days without moving them. Then turn the faucets on at full force and draw out two or three ounces in order to let the grains of lime pass out that may be in the faucet, carefully draw the water out slowly in demijohns and bottles. Keep the demijohns and bottles corked. The demijohns should be kept in a dry, cool place. And one faucet jar should be kept filled with this water for every day use. Those that practice this treatment of the above age, male or female, should keep their hair cut about one inch long for about the first nine months treatment. And should take a sponge bath twice daily for the first year, and after the first year the bath should be kept up at least once daily. The bath should be performed in this way: Put a washdish about one-third full of the wholesome water wash the face and head first and then wash downward and wash the feet last. Wipe with a coarse towel and brush the body over with a hair brush used for the head, except the head and feet. After about nine months treatment don't use the wholesome water on the head. If you have any sore places on the body and the wholesome water is too severe, do not wash such places with the wholesome water until healed, and if your hands are inclined to chap do not wash them with the wholesome water while chapped. The use of this water as aforesaid described causes the skin to be in a healthy condition. This water should be for drinking purposes for the first year's treatment.

When you cannot get the faucet jars made, use other jars instead, and dip the water out at the top. A drink of this water should be taken after each meal, and it is a good plan to take a drink before each meal. After the first year's use of this water only about half as much lime should be used. When this water cannot be had use boiled water without the lime, care being taken to never drink or apply raw water to the body when you can avoid it.

No. 3—SODA.

If your hands are inclined to chap, each day at bedtime put from one to two tablespoons of soda or as some term it, salaratus, in a wash dish and pour the washdish about one-third full of boiling water. Then when the water becomes cool enough wash the hands five or six minutes in the water and use it as hot as you can bear your hands in. Then rinse the hands in hot water without any soda in it. Wear gloves at night and as much as possible in the day time. Avoid working in wet weather or mud the first year.

No. 4—SORENESS.

If you have any sores, ulcers, or soreness in the outer portion of the rectum, groins or privates, each night at bedtime bathe the affected parts five or six minutes with the soda water No. 3, and use it as hot as you can bear it. This should be done just before the evening bath, and then rinse the same places with hot water without the soda.

No. 5—THE HEAD.

For cleaning the head, put about two tablespoonsfull of soda in a washdish and pour the washdish about one-half full of water and let it stand until it becomes partly cool. Then hold the head close to the washdish and wash it good with the water in the dish, then rinse through two or three waters and use it as hot as you can bear it. Then rinse the head with the iron solution and rinse again with hot water. Then with the cold boiled water wipe and comb the hair the usual way of combing your hair. The head should be washed as above described once a week. To some extent the hair feeds the mind, therefore it is necessary to take the proper care of it. The hair shoud be combed and brushed daily. After the first nine months treatment, when you desire to wet the hair use boiled water and never use any raw water on the head.

No. 6—BOILED WATER.

Boil the water as described in No. 2 and pour it in the faucetjars and let it set about two days, then draw out into demijohns and keep corked. After sixty days use of this water more should be boiled.

No. 7—IRON SOLUTION.

Put one-half of an ounce of sulphate of iron in a jar to every gallon of water you desire to add: Then boil the water and put it in the jar while hot, and let it set all night, and then empty the solution in demijohns, except sediments in the bottom, and keep corked. The eyes should be treated with this solution once a week. They should be bathed as described in the eye treatment No. 8. Then the face should be rinsed with hot water. When beginning to bathe the eyes in the above solution, reduce it with boiling water, and use it as hot as you can conveniently bear it. This solution is good for the rectum and womb. Use injections once a week. Force the solution out of the rectum by using the same exertion as it requires and action of the bowels. In case there is soreness in the rectum reduce the solution with the boiling water, then use an injection of warm water that has been boiled. If you have the piles and the outer portion of the rectum is inclined to be sore, wash it daily with this solution. The head should also be bathed with this solution after it has been washed as described in No. 5, and rinse good with hot water right away. The ears should be rinsed out with the solution from once to three times a week by way of an injection. I recommend the rectum syringe about four inches long for the ears. Wipe the ears out by folding a piece of white linen goods over the end of a holder made for that purpose. The holder should be about four inches long and about three-sixteenths of an inch in diameter, except at the end, which should be about one-eighth of an inch in diameter, and gradually slope back about one inch. A white linen handerkerchief that is partly worn is good to use on the holder. After the injection is made, fold the cloth over one end of the holder and put the end of the holder in the solution, then in the ear as far as it will enter without pressing too hard. Then rub the inside of the ear good on all sides, and as far as the holder will enter and continue this for three or four times by sticking the end of the holder in the solution each time. Then change the cloth on the holder and wipe the inside of the ears without putting the holder in the solution. Use the solution hot for the ears, or as hot as you can bear it. The syringe should be rinsed out with boiled water after using the iron solution. Once a week draw some of this solution up the nostrils until it comes in the mouth. Then wash the teeth good with the solution. Next wash the teeth with the wholesome water and use a hair brush. After this solution has been used about three months it should be made stronger, say about one ounce to a gallon of water. The unseen germ is the seat of almost all diseases. They cause the hair to turn gray and come out and penetrate to the brain and cause insanity. The iron solution is death to the unseen germs. Therefore if you treat the organs as described, it will prevent them from taking hold.

No. 8—EYE TREATMENT.

Put about one tablespoonful of salt in a washdish and pour the washdish about half-full of boiling water. Set the pan on a stool about two feet high, then set in a chair close to the stool and put your face in the water and let your forehead rest on the bottom of the dish. Draw your breath through your nose and continue to open and close your eyes for about four or five minutes in the water. Use the water as hot as you can. After you bathe the eyes as above for about one month then begin to add a little of the wholesome water to the salt water, just as your eyes can bear it. You might just cool the salt water with the wholesome water. This bathing should be kept up about twice daily the first year. Never cool the water with raw water. Avoid washing the face with raw water. After bathing the eyes the water in the wash dish should be poured in an extra jar and used for washing face or hands.

No. 9—MORNING TREATMENT.

Within one hour after the morning meal you should retire to your private closet and if an action of the bowels takes place use an injection with the boiled water and when you can add boiling water. Force out the water by exercising the same exertion that it requires to cause an action of the bowels. Then dip a piece of bleached muslin in the water and wipe the outer portion of the rectum. If there is no action of the bowels use the injection anyway, which will in all probability cause one. This way of treatment will in most cases cause a daily action of the bowels. I recommend the straight rectum syringe, one about seven inches long. Generally the surest place to find them is at a city drug store. At the same time females should treat the womb on the same principle. I recommend the straight rubber womb syringe for that purpose. About once a month draw a little melted hog's lard up the syringe, which will keep them in good condition. The teeth should also be washed after each meal, and whenevery any food is eaten between meals. They should be washed by using a brush in the wholesome water.

No. 10—CRUSHED SULPHATE OF IRON.

One No. 3 capsule of this iron should be taken daily after the morning made for five months from the time you begin treatment. This remedy is sure death to the unseen germs that are in the blood and entire system, and causes them to pass out in the way of pimples, carbuncles.. In case some become afflicted with carbuncles, they should treat themselves as near as possible that all of the corruption would pass out. The proper way to treat them is to add a little of the boiled castor oil to a thin slice of bacon and bind it on, and in bad cases they should be squeezed about every two hours and washed good with boiled water. In hot weather they should be dressed every two hours, except during the hours of sleep, with the wholesome water used cold. The slice of bacon should be placed in a dish of hot water before applied. This way of treatment should be kept up until the carbuncle about quits running. In case there is no carbuncle come on your body for a month or two after you begin treatment, take one of the capsules soon after the morning meal and one at bedtime until they create the desired effect, and then drop off to one after the morning meal. If the treatment causes carbuncles to come on your body to an extent that they are too severe to very well endure them, leave off the iron treatment for a few days. The above treatment causes the excrement to be of a darkish color, but it is no bad sign. None can expect to become in proper health to an extent that they can live for hundreds of years unless they are treated in a way so the dead bodies of the unseen germs pass out of the system. They are the main cause of short life while in the system, either dead or alive.

A teaspoonful of the oil No. 11 should be taken every evening awhile before bedtime during the iron treatment and until the bowels become in a healthy condition.

No. 11—BOWEL REMEDY.

Put castor oil in a pan and set on a hot stove until it comes to a boiling heat, then set the pan of oil off. When it becomes partly cool empty it into a bottle and keep it corked. This oil should be used to regulate the bowels and should be taken at bedtime in doses from one to three teaspoonsful when costive. The bowels should be regulated so a daily action takes place soon after the morning meal. This oil is good in case of piles.

No. 12—FIRST STAGE OF COLD AND LA GRIPPE.

Put one quart of cider vinegar in a stew cup. If cider vinegar cannot be had, other vinegar will do. Flavor with pepper and salt, then add a small piece of butter, a piece of alum about one-half an inch square. Set the cup on a hot stove, and when it comes to a boil set it off and let it become partly cool, then strain it into a quart bottle. During day time and when awake at night, take a little sup of this stew whenever you cough, or about every half hour. Your sleeping place should be in a room where there is a stove or fireplace. There should be enough fire kept up to keep out dampness. At bedtime, for one or two nights, take from one to five ounces of whisky or brandy, and wash off with the wholesome water, and keep well wrapped up during the hours of sleep. In bad cases, you should wash off every two hours, when awake, with the wholesome water, and use it cold. Wipe dry with a coarse towel. This bathing should be kept up until the cold is broken. Always spit out the phlegm; never swallow it.

No. 13—HAIR OINTMENT.

This ointment should not be used until after the first nine months treatment. Put one ounce of vaseline and one-fourth of an ounce of coaloil in a stew cup and set on a hot stove. When it comes to a boil set off and when it becomes partly cool pour the ointment into a large mouthed bottle and keep it corked.

When the hair is grey or of a dead nature, use a little of the ointment on the hair, but don't apply it too often, for the reason it might cause the hair to come out, but moderate use will do no harm. While using this ointment the head should be kept clean by washing as described in No. 5.

No. 14—POISON OAK.

Put hog's lard in a small pan and set it on a hot stove. When it comes to a kind of a boil apply it to the affected places for 10 or 15 minutes, and use it hot. If it burns the skin slightly it's all the better. Then wash the grease off with the hot soda water. Then wash off all over with the wholesome water and put on a change of underwear that has no coloring in them, something like bleach muslin.

No. 15—HOP POISON.

Apply the wholesome water three or four times daily to the parts affected.

No. 16.

Parties practicing this treatment, married or single, should avoid sexual abuse. Those over exerting themselves by the practice of sexual abuse can not expect to prolong life to any great extent. Children begin this practice when quite young, and it gradually grows on them until it becomes a disease to an extent that they cannot very well control their passions; and it is the same way with married people. To quite an extent parents are to blame for this evil. They should teach their children the danger of this evil before it becomes too late. There should be a course of study taught in the daily schools in regard to this evil. This abuse causes insanity, weakness and other diseases. Sometimes married people draw the idea that they are afflicted with some terrible disease, when it is merely a complaint brought on by sexual over-exertion. Those in that condition should take a trip to some distant country, and, by consent of their companions, remain away for ten or twenty years. We might consider that it would be the best medicine that they could take, and we might also consider people of that kind are digging their own graves. In such cases it is either early death, or stay away from companions. Those practicing this treatment should not over-exert themselves in any way by overwork or working too long in a day, losing sleep at night, by excessive drinking, drunkenness or lifting hard. Neither should they over-tax the brain by allowing the mind to dwell on one thing too long at a time. Some over-tax the brain by reading the heathen bibles. They draw the idea that it is their religious duty to perform certain acts or work in this life in order to be saved in the future. Such men are led away into fanaticism similar to Guitau, the assassinator of Garfield. Our actions in this life make no change in the world to come, and this world will never be fully civilized until priestcraft is abolished and laws based on principles of civilization as laid down in this book. Parties practicing this system should take daily exercise. I recommend out-door exercise for summer, and in-door exercise in damp weather. The ventilation for all sleeping rooms should be on a plan so the rooms could be ventilated, and in the summer season the sleeping rooms should be ventilated to an extent that it would be almost like sleeping in an open shed. It is better to sleep under plenty of covers when necessary to keep you warm and not depend too much on a warm room. Never sleep with your head elevated above the level of your body. Let your legs be stretched out most of the time. Make a practice of lying on either side or back, and do not make a practice of remaining awake at night.

Many people have their residence, barn and other buildings and well in a condition that the filth creates disease. I will describe how a building and location should be arranged among farmers at the present time. The following is subject to changes to suit circumstances and localities: First, select the building location on reasonably dry land and lay off the amount of land you want for all of the buildings. Plow the land one way by turning gee until you have raised it some higher in the center. Even it up and leave it a little lower at the outer edge and then make an open ditch deep enough to drain the surface water off, and in low or wet land put in sufficient tiling to drain the land. Build the residence on the side joining the public road and enclose it with a fence sufficient to keep out pigs, poultry and stock of every kind. The parlor, or front portion of the residence, should face the road, and if the residence is made of wood, it should be set a foot or two above the ground. The space below the residence should be closed with screen work. Each room of the residence should be made on a plan so they could be well ventilated and should always be kept clean. The barn, sty and chicken house should be on the opposite side of the described location from the road. The general water closet should be made with a seat, and a door to open under the seat from the outside of the closet. Buckets should be used for the purpose of setting under a seat. These buckets should hold about five gallons. A small lot should join the said closet, divided into two departments. The droppings that fall in the buckets should be spread on the ground of one of the said departments at a time and spaded under, and vegetables should be raised on one of the departments each year and fed to stock or poultry. No cesspools nor underground cellars should be on the premises. A well should be between the residence, barn and other buildings, on the following plan:

The well should be walled up with either stone or brick from the bottom to about three feet above the level of the ground and cemented on both sides from top to bottom, and the dirt around the well for twenty feet square should be made a little higher than the level of the ground and cemented. No buildings should be closer than fifteen feet of the well. The portion of the wall above the ground should be covered over with screen work. No roof should be over the well. There should be a picket fence around the cement sufficient to keep out poultry or stock of all kinds. An iron pump should be used for drawing the water. There should be sufficient hose to reach all the buildings with water. The stable and all outer buildings should be on a plan so as to be cleansed with water when necessary. The manure and waste straw should not be allowed to accumulate in or around any of the buildings on said location. The entire farm should be well drained with ditches and tiling when necessary. All underwear, clothing, handkerchiefs, ear schwabs, towels, bedclothing, or any clothes worn next to the body, should be rinsed in boiling water when washed. Jars, bottles, demijohns, buckets, dishes, or anything of that nature, should be kept clean and scalded out with boiling water when washed. It would be a benefit to feed cattle, sheep and hogs three months on boiled food and not be allowed to drink any water excepting what has been boiled, before butchered or slaughtered. That way of feeding stock would make their flesh much healthier for food. Milch cows should be fed on the same principle when in use.

No. 17.

I advise those that desire to practice this entire system to properly prepare things before beginning. A cellar and private closet should be made adjoining your sleeping room, and plenty of the water and everything necessary for the treatment should be kept on hand in the cellar so you would not be apt to neglect any part of the treatment. A good principle on which to build a cellar is as follows: Construct a wooden building eight by eight feet in the clear, with double walls about one foot apart and fill in with sawdust between the walls. Have the building a foot or so above the ground and make ventilators to come up under the floor and with a ventilator on top. A stove should be kept in the bedroom and in damp weather a fire should be built and the room warmed up before the morning or evening bath. The private closet should be on the plan as described in paragraph 18 in this department. I do not claim that all who practice this system can make a complete success at the start, but any one who observes the rules can be benefited, and if they keep it up life can be prolonged to an extent that some can live hundredes of years at the present age of the world. I will not be responsible in any way for any one's acts in following this treatment, for the reason that many would not go according to the described treatment and then if they failed to make a success some of them would probably lay the blame to me. It takes perseverance, patience and practice to be able to strictly follow the above rules. But those who strictly follow those rules will not be troubled with the disease that causes short life. The day of cancers, gray hair, false teeth, deafness, spectacles and short life will not exist to any great extent.

I recommend this treatment to those who have charge of asylums for the treatment of lunatics. The unseen germs is the principal cause of insanity. They enter the brain. For the treatment of lunatics the most of them should be limited to one meal per day for about three months, and then be allowed to eat the morning meal and a lunch during the day, not later than five o'clock p. m. The remainder of the treatment should be practiced as near as possible.

No. 18.

The healing institute for the purpose of treating disease in the way of prolonging life might be built in different ways. It could be built as below described, or made round with winding stairs in the center, and made either of stone or wood, but in either case the sleeping rooms should be on the outer portion of the building. The below is one way it might be built. A ten story building, about forty-five by forty-five feet, made of stone, each story ten feet in the clear. The first floor should be used for the superintendent's office and for a daily treatment room. The next eight floors above should be divided into rooms ten by twelve feet in the clear, and an eight foot gangway should be through the center of these floors, making a row of three rooms on each side of the gangway, and leaving a space of ten feet for elevators. This plan leaves a floor four by ten feet on the out side of each room. A door should lead from each room to the gangway and one from each room to the outside floor, and in the outer partition wall there should be private closets arranged with a door to open in the room, and a door should open on the outer floor under the seat. It should be made on a plan so that vessels could be set under the seat for the excrement to fall in. The vessels should be cleaned daily, and oftener when necessary. There should be a cistern under the building about six by twelve feet, about two to five hundred feet deep. It should be walled up about twenty feet with stone and arched over the top of the walls. A water pipe should lead from the bottom of the cistern to the tenth floor of the building, and the space above the wall should be filled up and finished on a plan so surface water could not seep through. There should be a pump on the tenth floor for the purpose of pumping water from the cistern, and a furnace for the purpose of boiling water and preparing it for use. Sufficient water pipes should lead from the tenth floor to all the rooms in the building and on the grounds. There should be a bath tub and bed, besides necessary fixtures for treatment, in each room, and the rooms should be on a plan so they could be well ventilated. Different germs exist in the lower atmosphere and the surface of water. These germs principally cause the surface water to become diseased, therefore it is necessary to go below where they exist, for water and draw it through tight pipes, partly above their existence, before used. The enclosure of the institute, when not built in the city, should extend over about ten acres of ground and be arranged similar to a park and should contain a bicycle track near the outer edge. On the outer edge of this tract of land there should be cottages convenient for families and single people. There should be a hotel on the grounds near the institute of sufficient size to care for all the inmates. The proper place to build an institute is on a hill or mountain. Parties practicing this treatment when opportunity affords, should reside at an institute of this kind from three months to five years; it's owing to the age and complaint. By so doing you would learn the rules of treatment proper. which would be a benefit all your life.

Greetings.

No. 1—THE GREAT KING.

The great King has come,
He's with us to-day,
To lead us by the hand
And cheer us on the way.

    Hallelluiah, O glory,
    Halleluiah, Oh men;
    Halleluiah, O glory,
    O glory to His name.

The great King has come;
He's with us to-day;
To lead us by the hand
And prolong our days.

    Halleluiah, O glory,
    Halleluiah, Oh men;
    Halleluiah, O glory.
    O glory to His name.

The great King has come,
He's with us to-day,
To lead us by the hand
And make a home for man.

    Halleluiah, O glory,
    Halleluiah, Oh men.
    Halleluiah, O glory.
    O glory to His name.

No. 2—LET US WALK.

Let us walk with the Saviour
For God has sent us a gift,
Let us walk with the Saviour.
Such a gift is the gift of love.

Let us walk with the Saviour,
Such a gift prolongs our days.
Let us walk with the Saviour,
And thank God for such a gift.

No. 3—SALVATION ARMY.

I belong to the Salvation Army,
I know the Saviour's come;
For we march through the city
With a great big drum.

I belong to the Salvation Army,
And I know He came to stay,
For we march through the city
And tell the people so.

I belong to the Salvation Army,
And I know He came to dwell,
For He marches through the city
Of the great west.

We are going west, we are going west,
We are going west to Him there,
Our captain, O our captain dear,
Our captain, O our captain, dear

When we get there and see His face,
We'll then thank God for such a gift,
Our Captain, O our captain, dear.
Our captain, O our captain, dear

No. 4—GREAT PHYSICIAN.

This Great Physician, now on earth.
The same loving Saviour;
He leads the drooping by the hand.
The same loving Saviour.

Sweetest words I ever heard.
Sweetest ways I ever saw.
Sweetest songs I ever sung.
The same loving Saviour.

No. 5—O, GLORY.

O glory, the Saviour of man has come;
The blind will see, the deaf will hear,
The dumb will speak, the lame will walk.
O, glory, glory to His name.

O glory, He has come to stay
The blind will see, the deaf will hear,
The dumb will speak, the lame will walk;
O glory, glory to His name.

O glory, He has come to dwell.
The blind will see, the deaf will hear,
The dumb will speak, the lame will walk,
O glory, glory to His name.

No. 6—GOLDEN SHEAVES.

Sowing in the daytime,
Sowing seeds of knowledge,
Sowing in the evening,
And in the dewy morn.

Now's the time of harvest.
And the time of reaping;
He's on earth rejoicing.
Gathering up the sheaves.

Gathering in the golden sheaves,
Gathering in the golden sheaves,
He's on earth rejoicing
Gathering up the sheaves.

No. 7—O, NOW.

O now I see the old, old Saviour
Who was once among men;
It satisfies my longings
To see Him here again.

O. the old, old Saviour,
He's with us here to-day,
To reap the great, great harvest,
At God's own command.

No. 8—COME TO JESUS.

Come to Jesus, come to Jesus,
For it's God's own design;
Come to Jesus, come to Jesus,
For it's God's own command.

Come to Jesus, come to Jesus,
For it's God's great plan;
Come to Jesus, come to Jesus,
And prolong your days.

No. 9—SEE THOSE CLOUDS.

See those clouds a hanging there?
See those coluds up in the sky?
When will those clouds disappear?
When will the sun shine again?

If those clouds will pass away,
And the sun will shine again,
We will unite as one
And help remove the land.

See those clouds a hanging there?
See those clouds up in the sky,
When will those clouds disappear?
When will the sun shine again?

If those clouds will pass away,
And the sun will shine again,
We will all join hands
And help to save mankind.

No. 10—TO CHILDREN.

Come, little children, meet your Saviour,
Come and meet him now;
I'll receive you, I will love you,
I will teach you how to do.

How to love your mama and your papa too,
Yes, I love you, love to teach you how to do.
Love to teach you how to love your sisters
And your brother, and all mankind, too.

No. 11—CHILDREN'S REPLY.

O, dear Saviour, how we love you,
How we love to meet you, too.
How we love you because you told us how to do
How to love our mama and our papa, too.

Yes, dear Saviour, we do love you,
Because you told us how to do.
How to love our sister and our brother,
And all mankind, too.

No. 11—SAMBO.

O Sambo, let's work the 'taters and hoe the corn.
For old massa has come to dwell a second time.
O Sambo, let's work the 'taters and hoe the corn,
For old massa has come to dwell one thousand years.

O Sambo, let's work the 'taters and hoe the corn,
For old massa has come to remove the land.
O Sambo, let's work the 'taters and hoe the corn,
For old massa has come to save mankind.

No. 12—WHEN WILL.

O Saviour, when will you come to dwell with us?
Our home is across the wide ocean.
O Saviour, when will you come to lead us the way?
Our homes is across the wide ocean.

O Saviour, when will you unite us as one?
Our homes is across the wide ocean.
O Saviour, when will you prolong our days?
Our homes is across the wide ocean.

No. 13—CRUCIFIXION.

What did the heathen do with the Saviour?
O, what did the heathen do with the Saviour?
What did the heathens do with the Saviour?
When he was first on earth?

They led him away in open shame.
They led him away in open shame,
They led him away in open shame.
And crucified Him.

What will the people do with the Saviour?
What will the people do with the Saviour?
What will the people do with the Saviour?
At His second call.

O, let us all receive Him,
O, let us all receive Him,
O, let us all receive Him,
At this second call.

No. 14—THE MARCH.

We are marching along, we are marching along.
We are marching along to Paradise.
The Saviour's come, the Saviour's come,
The Saviour's come from God's great throne.

We are marching along, we are marching along,
We are marching along to Paradise:
He came to stay, He came to stay.
He came to stay to lead mankind the way.

We are marching along, we are marching along.
We are marching along to Paradise:
He came to dwell, He came to dwell,
He came to dwell to save mankind as well.

No. 15—ROBERT INGERSOLL.

A gift from God, a gift of love.
A gift to Robert Ingersoll.
A gift from God, a gift to man.
A gift of one thousand years.

My Saviour dwells within the west.
Far, far beyond the rocky hills,
I'm going west, I'm going west,
I'm going west to meet Him there.

When I get there and see His face,
I'll then thank God for righteousness.
I'm going west, I'm going west.
I'm going west to meet Him there.

No. 16—IN THE LIGHT.

O, let us gather with the Saviour,
O, let us gather with the Saviour,
O, let us gather with the Saviour,
As he was here before.

He has come to gather
His fold to him once more.
Let us walk in the light
Let us walk in the light of God.

No. 17—THE OLD SHEPHERD.

God's great day has come at last.
The old shepherd has arrived.
When will the old flock come home
To meet the old shepherd again?

When will the old flock come home
To lie down in the fold?
When will the old flock come home
To learn of him the way?

When will the old flock come home
To learn of God's great day?
When will the old flock come home
To help remove the land?

No. 18—HER BODY.

Her body now dwells within the tomb.
Her mind now rests in peace with God;
Her earthly days have now gone by
Her mind dwells in peace with God.

We will meet her, we will meet her.
We will meet her on the other shore.
We will meet her, we will meet her.
We will meet her on the other shore.

We will now depart and leave the tomb.
But when our earthly days go by.
We will then unite with her again.
When we meet on the other shore.

No. 19—HIS PRESENT.

His present home is in God's throne.
Far beyond his earthly home.
With joy and peace we'll meet him there,
In God's great throne we'll meet him there.

When we get there and see his face.
We'll then thank God for such a place.
We'll meet him there, we'll meet him there.
We'll meet him on the other shore.

All earthly joys have now gone by,
But he's with peace in God's great throne,
We'll meet him there, we'll meet him there,
We'll meet him on the other shore.

No. 20—I HAVE SEEN.

I have seen Him here to-day.
He's just the same Jesus.
I am glad to meet Him here.
He's just the same Jesus.

He has come with us to stay.
He's just the same Jesus.
And lead mankind the way.
He's just the same Jesus.

No. 21—A HOME.

This world should be a world of love.
And we should do as God commands.
For God has sent one from Its throne
To dwell on earth one thousand years.

This world should be a world of love.
And we should do as God commands.
For God has sent one from Its throne
To dwell on earth a second time.

This world should be a world of love,
And we should do as God commands,
For God has sent one from Its throne
To dwell on earth to save mankind.

No. 22—HALLELUIAH.

Halleluliah, Halleluiah,
The Saviour of man has come.
Halleluliah, Halleluiah,
He came to lead mankind the way.
Halleluiah, Halleluiah,
He came to prolong our days;
Halleluiah, Halleluiah,
He came to save mankind as well.

No. 23—GLORY.

O glory, O glory,
The Saviour of man has come.
O glory, O glory,
He came to lead mankind the way.
O glory, O glory,
He came to prolong our days.
O glory, O glory,
He came to save mankind as well.

No. 24—JUBILEE.

O Jubilee, Jubilee, glory,
The Saviour of man is on earth;
O Jubilee, Jubilee, glory,
He has come to set mankind free.
O Jubilee, Jubilee, glory,
He has come to prolong our days;
O Jubilee, Jubilee, glory,
He has come to save mankind, too.

No. 25—REMOVE THE LAND.

There's only one way to remove the land,
And that is to join the Saviour's band.
There's only one way to remove the land,
And that is to join the Saviour's church.

GREETINGS. 61

There's only one way to remove the land,
And that is to unite as one,
There's only one way to remove the land,
And that is to accept God's great plan.

No. 26—WHAT WOULD.

What would this world be without Jesus
To lead mankind the way?
What would this world be without Jesus
To unite mankind as one.

What would this world be without Jesus
To prolong our days?
What would this world be without Jesus
To remove the land.

What would this world be without Jesus
To make a home for man.
To save mankind?
What would this world be without Jesus

No. 27—TO MARCH THE WORLD ALONG.

O when will we get through singing the Saviour's songs.
For they just keep coming right along.
O when will we get through singing the Saviour's songs.
For He will dwell one thousand years.

O when will we get through singing the Saviour's songs.
For God sent them to prolong our days.
O when will we get through singing the Saviour's songs.
For God sent them to march the world along.

O when will we get through singing the Saviour's songs.
For God sent them to remove the land.
O when will we get through singing the Saviour's songs.
For God sent them to save mankind.

No. 28—SEE JESUS.

You can now see Jesus
And dwell with Him on land,
And drink the flowing fountain
By God's own design.

You can now see Jesus,
And dwell with Him on land,
And drink the flowing fountain
By God's own command.

You can now see Jesus,
And dwell with Him on land,
And drink the flowing fountain
By God's great plan.

You can now see Jesus,
And dwell with Him on land,
And drink the flowing fountai
To unite mankind.

No. 29—THE ELEPHANT.

The world has an elephant on its hands,
For the Saviour has come to make new plans.
The world has an elephant on its hands
For He has come to unite the world as one.

The world has an elephant on its hands,
For He has come to coin the money twenty to one,
The world has an elephant on its hands,
For He has come to remove the land.

The world has an elephant on its hands,
For He has come by God's command,
The world has an elephant on its hands,
For He has come to dwell one thousand years.

No. 30—JOLLY TIME.

This world should be a jolly world,
And we should have a jolly time.
For God has sent one from Its throne.
To dwell on earth one thousand years.

This world should be a jolly world,
And we should have a jolly time.
For God has sent one from Its throne.
To dwell on earth a second time.

This world should be a jolly world,
And we should have a jolly time,
For God has sent one from Its throne,
To make this world a home for man.

This world should be a jolly world,
And we should have a jolly time,
For God has sent one from Its throne,
To dwell on earth to save mankind.

No. 31—WALK WITH JESUS.

O come and walk with Jesus
And make this world a world of love;
O come and walk with Jesus
And make this world a world of joy.

O come and walk with Jesus
And make this world as God designs,
O come and walk with Jesus
And make this world as God commands.

O come and walk with Jesus
And make this world on God's great plan;
O come and walk with Jesus
And make this world a home for man.

No. 32—LET'S LAY ASIDE.

Let's lay aside all malice and unite as one,
Let's lay aside all malice and join the Saviour's band.
Let's lay aside all malice and remove the land.
Let's lay aside all malice and help save mankind.

No. 33—O WON'T.

O won't it be joyful when the world joins the Saviour's band
And unite as one.
O won't it be joyful when the world joins the Saviour's band
To remove the land.

O won't it be joyful when the world joins the Saviour's band
To divide the high sea.
O won't it be joyful when the world joins the Saviour's band
To make a home for man.

O won't it be joyful when the world joins the Saviour's band
To help to save mankind.
O won't it be joyful when the world joins the Saviour's band
To build the great city on land.

No. 34—EARTHLY HOME.

I love this earthly home of ours,
For God has sent a Saviour to dwell.
I love this earthly home of ours,
For God has sent the Saviour to unite us as one.

I love this earthly home of ours,
For God has sent the Saviour to prolong our days,
I love this earthly home of ours,
For God has sent the Saviour to remove the land.

I love this earthly home of ours,
For God has sent the Saviour to make a home for man.
I love this earthly home of ours,
For God has sent the Saviour to save mankind.

No. 35—O WHEN.

O when will the Saviour meet us at home?
O when will He come to unite us as one?
O when will the Saviour meet us at home?
O when will He come to lead us the way?

O when will the Saviour meet us at home?
O when will He come to prolong our days?
O when will the Saviour meet us at home?
O when will we learn of God's great day?

No. 36—O, THERE.

O there's many waiting, O there's many waiting,
For the old shepherd to return.
O there's many waiting, O there's many waiting,
On the other shore.

O there's many waiting, O there's many waiting,
For the old shepherd to return.
O there's many waiting, O there's many waiting,
In God's great throne.

O there's many waiting, O there's many waiting,
For the old shepherd to return,
O there's many waiting, O there's many waiting,
On God's great shore.

O there's many waiting, O there's many waiting,
For the old shepherd to return,
O there's many waiting, O there's many waiting,
To meet Him once more.

No. 37—O COMPANION.

O companion, O companion,,
As we have lived in peace and love together
Let us join the Saviour's band,
And help unite mankind.

O companion, O companion,,
As we have lived in peace and love together
Let us join the Saviour's band,
And prolong our days.

O companion, O companion,,
As we have lived in peace and love together
Let us join the Saviour's band,
And help remove the land.

O companion, O companion,,
As we have lived in peace and love together
Let us join the Saviour's band,
And help make a home for man.

No. 38—DAY OF LOVE.

This is a day of love,
This is a day of peace and joy.
The Saviour come to lead us the way.
He meets all mankind.

He meets those who have been driven from their homes,
In shame and dismay.
He leads the drooping by the hand,
And cheers them on their way.

This is a day of love,
This is a day of peace and joy,
The Saviour come to unite us as one.
He meets all mankind.

He meets those who have been driven from their homes
In shame and dismay,
He leads the drooping by the hand,
And cheers them on their way.

No. 39—LOVE THAT.

O glory, the love that comes from God,
Gives us peace and joy.
O glory, the love that comes from God,
Leads mankind the way.

O glory, the love that comes from God,
Unites mankind as one.
O glory, the love that comes from God,
Is to all mankind.

No. 40—O JESUS.

O Jesus, O Saviour, such love I never endured,
O Jesus, O Saviour, such love I never enjoyed.
O Jesus, O Saviour, such love comes from God,
O Jesus, O Saviour, such love is to all mankind.

No. 41— O MAUDIE.

O Maudie, dear, O Maudie, O
You are too young to wed the boys;
But you can live at home in peace,
And make this world a world of love.

O Maudie, dear, O Maudie, O
You are too young to wed the boys;
But you can live at home in peace,
And make this world a world of joy.

O Maudie, dear, O Maudie, O
You are too young to wed the boys;
And you can soar on wings of love,
And fly across the wide ocean, too.

O Maudie, dear, O Maudie, O
You are too young to wed the boys;
You should well look before you leap,
Or you might land in trouble heap.

No. 42—O, SISTER, DEAR.

O. Sister, O, O, Sister, dear;
You are all alone with care,
But you can trust in God for righteousness,
And make your home a home of love.

O. Sister, O, O, Sister, dear;
You are all alone with care,
But you must trust n God for all your wants,
And make your home a home of joy.

O. Sister, O. O, Sister, dear;
You are all alone with care,
But you can live in peace and joy,
And trust in God for all your care.

O. Sister, O. O. Sister, dear;
You are all alone with care,
But you will soar on wings of love,
And land on the other shore.

No. 43—LITTLE BABY.

O little baby, dear little baby,
Sweet little baby I have come to you.
O little baby, dear little baby,
Sweet little baby, I have come to you now.

O little baby, dear little baby,
Sweet little baby, I love you, too
O little baby, dear little baby,
Sweet little baby, I love you now.

O little baby, dear little baby,
Sweet little baby, I receive you, too.
O little baby, dear little baby,
Sweet little baby, I receive you now.

No. 44—MILLENIUM.

O this great millenium day.
The Saviour of man is on earth.
O this great millenium day.
He has come to set mankind free.

O this great millenium day.
He has come to save mankind too.
O this great millenium day.
He has come to prolong our day.

No. 45—O LET'S.

O let's remove the land to the equator.
O let's remove the land.
O let's remove the land to the equator,
As God designs.

O let's remove the land to the equator,
O let's remove the land.
O let's remove the land to the equator,
As God commands.

O let's remove the land to the equator,
O let's remove the land.
O let's remove the land to the equator,
On God's great plan.

No. 46—LET'S LAY ASIDE.

O glory, let's lay aside the Jewish bible,
And receive the Saviour, O.
O glory, let's lay aside the Jewish bible,
And unite as one.

O glory, let's lay aside the Jewish bible,
And all join hands.
O glory, let's lay aside the Jewish bible,
And remove the land.

O glory, let's lay aside the Jewish bible,
And prolong our days.
O glory, let's lay aside the Jewish bible,
As God commands.

GREETINGS.

No. 47—GATHER.

Gather with the Saviour, do not delay.
Here by His word He is with us to-day,
And by His accent He's leading the way,
Tenderly pleading now.

Joyful, joyful is the meeting now,
And with joy we will now dwell with thee.
Yes, we will gather, Saviour, with thee,
In thy celestial home.

No. 48—O, HOW.

O how happy mankind should be
For God's great day here on earth.
It was made to set mankind free,
It was made to save mankind, too.

O how happy mankind should be,
For God's great day here on earth.
It was made for a Saviour of man,
It was made for the Saviour to lead.

O how happy mankind should be,
For God's great day here on earth.
It was made for the old Nazaree,
It was made to divide the high sea.

No. 49—WHEN WILL.

When will the old flock come home?
When will the old flock arrive?
When will the old flock come home?
And lie down in the fold.

When will the old flock come home?
When will the old flock arrive?
When will the old flock come home?
To learn of Him the way.

When will the old flock come home?
When will the old flock arrive?
When will the old flock come home?
To learn of God's great day.

No. 50—LAY ASIDE.

O glory, let's lay aside the Christian bible,
And receive the Saviour, O.
O glory, let's lay aside the Christian bible,
And unite as one.

O glory, let's lay aside the Christian bible,
And join all hands,
O glory, let's lay aside the Christian bible,
And remove the land.

O glory, let's lay aside the Christian bible,
And prolong our days.
O glory, let's lay aside the Christian bible,
As God commands.

No. 51—A REVOLUTION.

A revolution is coming,
A revolution is coming,
A revolution is coming,
And it will soon be here.

I now give you warning,
I now give you warning,
I now give you warning,
For it will soon be here.

The ball is now rolling,
The ball is now rolling,
The ball is now rolling,
And it will soon reach us.

Save your money, boys,
Save your money, O.
Save your money, boys,
To protect your home.

Let's lay aside our prejudice,
Let's lay aside our prejudice,
Let's lay aside our prejudice,
And unite as one.

Let's make more fleets,
Let's build more forts,
To protect the land
From the foreigners.

Let's make more fleets,
Let's build more forts,
To protect the land
Of the free and brave.

Let's make more fleets,
Let's build more forts,
To protect the land
Where the Saviour dwells.

No. 52—WHEN JESUS.

When Jesus came the second time
To dwell on earth one thousand years,
The heathen led Him from His home
And placed Him in a prison cell.

O what a shame, O what a shame,
To lead Him from His home and friends
O what a shame, O what a shame,
To rob Him of His liberty.

When Jesus came the second time
To dwell on earth to lay God's plan,
The heathen led Him from His home
And placed Him in a prison cell.

O what a shame, O what a shame,
To lead Him from His home and friends.
O what a shame, O what a shame,
To rob Him of His liberty.

When Jesus came the second time
To dwell on earth to save mankind,
The heathen led Him from His home,
And placed Him in a prison cell.

O what a shame, O what a shame,
To lead Him from His home and friends.
O what a shame, O what a shame,
To rob Him of His liberty.

No. 53—O DAUGHTER.

O daughter, daughter, daughter, dear;
O daughter, daughter, do come home.
I need your help, you need my care,
O daughter, daughter, do come home.

For God has sent one from Its throne
To dwell on earth one thosand years.
And He has come from God's great throne
To dwell on earth a second time.

Yes, He has come from God's great throne,
To dwell on earth to save mankind.
O daughter, daughter, daughter, dear,
O daughter, daughter, do come home.

No. 54—DAUGHTER'S REPLY.

I'm going home, I'm going home
I'm going home to see papa.
He needs my help, I need his care,
I'm going home to see papa.

For God has sent one from Its throne
To dwell on earth one thousand years.
And he has come from God's great throne,
To dwell on earth a second time.

He has come from God's great throne
To dwell on earth to save mankind.
I'm going home, I'm going home,
I'm going home to see papa.

No. 55—THOSE SONGS.

Those songs will never die,
Those songs will never die.
Those songs will always dwell
Which was composed by the Saviour of man.

Those songs will never die,
Those songs will never die,
Those songs will always dwell,
Which was composed by God's command.

Those songs will never die,
Those songs will never die,
Those songs will always dwell
Which was composed to lead mankind the way.

Those songs will never die,
Those songs will never die,
Those songs will always dwell
Which was composed to remove the land.

Those songs will never die,
Those songs will never die,
Those songs will always dwell
Which was composed to save mankind as well.

No. 56—THS DAY.

This day, this day,
This wonderful, wonderful day.
This day, this day,
This beautiful, beautiful day.

This day, this day,
This glorious, glorious day.
For God has sent the Saviour
To meet all mankind.

This day, this day.
This wonderful, wonderful day,
This day, this day,
This beautiful, beautiful day.

This day, this day,
This glorious, glorious day.
For one has come to dwell on earth,
Whose name was Nazaree.

This day, this day,
This wonderful, wonderful day.
This day, this day,
This beautiful, beautiful day.

This day, this day,
This glorious, glorious day,
For one has come from God's great throne
To dwell on earth one thousand years.

And He had come from God's great throne
To dwell on earth a second time.
Yes, He has come from God's great throne.
To dwell on earth to save mankind.

No. 57—O BLOW.

O blow the bugle,
O sound the trumpet.
O blow the bugle,
The Saviour of man has come.

O blow the bugle,
O sound the trumpet,
O blow the bugle,
The Saviour of man is on earth.

O blow the bugle,
O sound the trumpet.
O blow the bugle,
He has come by God's command.

O blow the bugle,
O sound the trumpet.
O blow the bugle,
He has come to save mankind.

No. 58—O THE LAMB.

O the lamb, O the lamb,
The precious lamb of God.
He has come, He has come.
To make us a gift.

O the lamb, O the lamb.
The precious lamb of God.
Such a gift, such a gift.
Prolongs our days.

O the lamb, O the lamb.
The precious lamb of God.
Such a gift, such a gift.
Was sent from God.

O the lamb, O the lamb.
The precious lamb of God.
Such a gift, such a gift.
Is to all mankind.

No. 59—CHEER UP.

Cheer up, Saviour; weep no more.
Bright days will come by and by.
We will unite as one,
And prolong our days.

Cheer up, Saviour; weep no more;
Bright days will come by and by.
We will help remove the land
To make a home for man.

No. 60—IT IS HIM.

It is Him, it is Him. it is Him.
He has come to make us a gift.
Such a gift prolongs our days.

It is Him, it is Him. it is Him.
He has come to make us a gift.
Such a gift was sent from God.

It is Him. it is Him. it is Him.
He has come to make us a gift,
Such a gift is to all mankind.

No. 61—OUR FRIEND.

Our friend has left her earthly home.
But she now dwells on the other shore.
We should all rejoice to know.

When our earthly days go by.
That we will meet her on the other shore.
And then we will unite again.

When we leave our home on land.
And dwell on the other shore.
We will meet her, we will meet her.

We will meet her and unite again.
We will meet her, we will meet her,
We will meet her and unite as one.

No. 62—HE'S JUST.

I have come to meet Him here.
I have come to see Him here.
He's just the Jesus.

I thank God for righteousness,
I thank God for such a gift.
He's just the same Jesus.

He has come to dwell on land.
He has come to see mankind.
He's just the same Jesus.

No. 63—A CHRISTIAN CHURCH.

I belong to a Christian Church.
And I'm glad the Saviour's come.
For He has come to unite mankind as one.

I belong to a Christian Church.
And I'm glad the Saviour's come.
For He has come to lead mankind the way.

I belong to a Christian Church.
And I'm glad the Saviour's come.
For He has come to dwell one thousand years.

No. 64—O MASSA.

O Massa, we will leave the land.
And dwell on some other shore.
If its God's own design.

GREETINGS.

O Massa, we will leave the land.
And dwell on some other shore.
If its God's own command.

O Massa, we will leave the land.
And dwell on some other shore.
If its God's great plan.

O Massa, we will leave the land.
And dwell on some other shore,
To help to save mankind.

No. 65—THE EAST.

O glory, let's soar on wings of love.
And fly to the great west.
And meet the Saviour there.

O glory, let's soar on wings of love.
And fly to the great west.
And lie down in the fold.

O glory, let's soar on wings of love.
And fly to the great west,
And learn of Him the way.

O glory, let's soar on wings of love.
And fly to the great west,
And learn of God's great day.

No. 66—O HOW.

O how happy we will be, O now happy we will be,
When we land on the other shore.
And meet our friends who have gone before.

O how happy we will be, O how happy we will be,
When we land on the other shore.
And dwell on land where God we'll see.

No. 67—O DAISY.

O Daisy, sweetheart,
There's a love that comes from God.
To unite us as one.

O Daisy, sweetheart,
There's a love that comes from God,
To give us peace and poy.

There's a love that comes from God,
Let us now unite as one,
And help to save mankind.

No. 68—O LET'S.

O let's unite with the Saviour,
And receive the love of God,
And unite mankind as one.

O let's unite with the Saviour,
And receive the love of God,
And prolong our days.

O let's unite with the Saviour.
And receive the love of God,
And remove the land.

O let's unite with the Saviour,
And receive the love of God.
And help save mankind.

No. 69—LOVE FROM GOD.

Halleluiah, Halleluiah, O glory,
There is a love that comes from God.
That gives us peace of mind.

Halleluiah, Halleluiah, O glory,
There is a love that comes from God,
To lead mankind the way.

Halleluiah, Halleluiah, O glory.
There is a love that comes from God,
To unite mankind as one.

Halleluiah, Halleluiah, O glory,
There is a love that comes from God
To save mankind as well.

No. 70—LOVE ALL MANKIND.

O glory, God's love is resting on me,
O glory, it gives me peace of mind.
O glory it leads me by the hand.

O glory, it comes to prolong our days.
O glory it comes to remove the land.
O glory, it comes to save mankind.

No. 71—A LAND OF.

There is a land of love,
There is a land of peace and joy,
Of which we will return.

There is a land of love,
There is a land of peace and joy,
Of which the Saviour once dwelt.

There is a land of love,
There is a land of peace and joy.
Of which the Saviour will return.

There is a land of love,
There is a land of peace and joy,
Of which the Saviour will meet us again.

No. 72—THE OLD.

Halleluiah, O glory, the old shepherd has arrived.
Halleluiah, O glory, the old flock is coming home
To lie down in the fold.

Halleluiah, O glory, the old shepherd has arrived.
Halleluiah, O glory, the old flock is coming home
To learn him the way.

Halleluiah, O glory, the old shepherd has arrived.
Halleluiah, O glory, the old flock is coming home
To learn of God's great day.

No. 73—WAKE UP, GIRLS.

Wake up, girls, and sleep no longer,
The dawn of day is breaking.
The Saviour of man is on land.

Wake up, girls, and sleep no longer,
The dawn of day is breaking,
He has come to set you free.

Wake up, girls, and sleep no longer,
The dawn of day is breaking,
He has come to wed you, too.

No. 74—O WHAT FUN.

O what fun the boys will now have.
For the Saviour of man is on land.
O what fun the boys will now have,

For He came to set mankind free.
O what fun the boys will now have.
For he has come to dwell a thousand years.

No. 75.—HALLELUIAH.

Halleluiah, jubilee; Halleluiah, jingle,
Halleluiah, glory Halleluiah, boom, boom, boom,
The Saviour of man has come.

Halleluiah, jubilee; Halleluiah, jingle,
Halleluiah, glory Halleluiah, boom, boom, boom,
He has come to set mankind free.

No. 76—THERE IS.

There is showers of blessings,
There is showers of blessings,
Such blessings come from God.

There is showers of blessings,
There is showers of blessings,
To lead mankind the way.

There is showers of blessings,
There is showers of blessings,
To unite mankind as one.

There is showers of blessings,
There is showers of blessings,
Which is to all mankind.

No. 77—FREE THINKERS.

We are glad that the Saviour
Rejected the Christian bible,
And has come to set mankind free.

We are glad that the Saviour
Rejected the Jewish bible,
And has come to save mankind too.

No. 78—GOD'S GREAT.

God's great day has come,
All mankind should unite as one,
And prolong their days.

God's great day has come,
All mankind should unite as one.
And help remove the land.

No. 79—HALLELUIAH.

Halleluiah, Halleluiah, O glory,
Let's all rejoice, let's all weep with joy,
For the savior of man has come.

Halleluiah, Halleluiah, O glory,
Let's all rejoice, let's all weep with joy.
For He has come to dwell one thousand years.

Halleluiah, Halleluiah, O glory,
Let's all rejoice, let s all weep with joy.
For He has come to prolong our days.

No. 80—O GLORY.

O glory, when will the world unite in one great band
And receive the Saviour, O?
O glory, glory to His name.

O glory, when will the world unite in one great band
And learn of Him the way?
O glory, glory to His name.

O glory, when will the world unite in one great band
And help remove the land?
O glory, glory to His name.

O glory, when will the world unite in one great band
And make a home for man?
O glory, glory to his name.

O glory, when will the world unite in one great band,
And help to save mankind;
O glory, glory to His name.

No. 81—THE WORLD.

O glory, the world will weep, the world will wail,
For the Saviour of man is on earth.
Halleluiah. O glory, glory to His name.

O glory, the world will weep, the world will wail,
For He has come to dwell one thousand ears.
Halleluiah. O glory, glory to His name.

O glory, the world will weep, the world will wail,
For He has come to prolong our days.
Halleluiah. O glory, glory to His name.

No. 82—HALLELUIAH.

Halleluiah, O glory, for a home on earth.
Halleluiah, O glory, such a home comes from God.
Halleluiah, O glory, such a home prolongs our days.

Halleluiah, O glory, such a home saves mankind.
Halleluiah, O glory, such a home is to all mankind.
Haleluiah, O glory, we thank God for such a home.

No. 83—O COME.

O come and join the Saviour's band,
And unite the world as one.
On money just twenty to one.

O come and join the Saviour's band,
And lead mankind the way.
O money, just twenty to one.

O come and join the Saviour's band.
And prolong your days,
On money just twenty to one.

No. 84—WHEN WILL.

When will the world weep?
When will the world rejoice?
Over the Saviour, O.

When will the world weep?
When will the world rejoice?
Over God's great plan.

When will the world weep?
When will the world rejoice?
And unite as one?

When will the world weep?
When will the world rejoice?
And remove the land?

No. 85—O COME AND JOIN.

O come and join the Saviour's church,
O come and join the Saviour's band,
And unite as one.

O come and join the Saviour's church,
O come and join the Saviour's band,
And learn of Him the way.

O come and join the Saviour's church,
O come and join the Saviour's band,
And learn of God's great day.

No. 86—O COME, COME.

O come, come, come and meet the Saviour,
While He is here on earth,
For we will meet Him in God's great throne.

O come, come, come and meet the Saviour,
While He is here on earth,
For we will see Him in God's great throne.

O come, come, come and meet the Saviour,
While He is here on earth,
For He will lead us in God's great throne.

No. 87—HEATHEN BIBLES.

O destroy your heathen bibles,
And your heathen books.
And get ready for the Saviour, O.

O destroy your heathen bibles,
And your heathen books.
And prepare your chaples for the Saviour too.

O destroy your heathen bibles,
And your heathen books.
And except the great plan that God has took.

No. 88—A HOME.

A home on earth, a home of love,
Which is a gift from God.

A home on earth, it is a gift
Which gift prolongs our days.

A home on earth it came from God,
Which gives us peace and joy.

No. 89—TURN.

Roll the ball, turn the wheel,
The Saviour has come.

Roll the ball, turn the wheel,
He came to stay.

Roll the ball, turn the wheel,
To lead mankind the way.

Roll the ball, turn the wheel,
He came to dwell.

Roll the ball, turn the wheel.
To save mankind as well.

No. 90—JINGLE..

Jingle, Jingle, boom, boom,
The Saviour of man has come.

Jingle, Jingle, boom, boom.
He came to stay.

Jingle, Jingle, boom, boom.
To lead mankind the way.

Jingle, Jingle, boom, boom.
He came to dwell.

Jingle, Jingle, boom, boom.
To save mankind as well.

No. 91—O, O, O.

O, O, O, chow, chow, chow,
Melican man's God has come.

O, O, O, chow, chow, chow,
Him comee to set mankind free.

O, O, O, chow, chow, chow,
Him comee to save mankind too.

O, O, O, chow, chow, chow,
Him comee to prolong our days.

O, O, O, chow, chow, chow,
Him comee to dwell one thousand years.

No. 92—COME ALONG.

Come along, friends, and go to Jesus.
And lie down in the fold.

Come along, friends, and go to Jesus.
And learn of Him the way.

Come along, friends, and go to Jesus,
And learn of God's great day.

Come along, friends, and go to Jesus,
To unite mankind as one.

No. 93—I WILL ARISE.

I will arise and go to Jesus,
And lie down in the fold.

I will arise and go to Jesus,
And learn of Him the way.

I will arise and go to Jesus,
To learn of God's great day.

I will arise and go to Jesus,
To unite mankind as one.

No. 94—LET'S ALL.

The Saviour's come, the Saviour's come,
O let's all join in and unite as one.

The Saviour's come, the Saviour's come,
O let's all join in and divide the high sea.

The Saviour's come, the Saviour's come,
O let's all join in and help remove the land.

No. 95—O, JESUS.

O Jesus, O Jesus, this should be a world of love,
For one has come to dwell.

O Jesus, O Jesus, this should be a world of love,
For one has come to stay.

O Jesus, O Jesus, this should be a world of love,
For one has come to roam.

No. 96—MUST JESUS.

Must Jesus do the work alone,
And lead mankind the way?

Must Jesus do the work alone,
And unite mankind as one.

Must Jesus do the work alone,
And prolong our days.

Must Jesus do the work alone,
And remove the land?

Must Jesus do the work alone,
And all the world go free?

O there's a work for every one,
And there's a crown for you.

No. 97—WE'LL NEVER.

We'll never forget the time,
When the Saviour come to dwell on land.

We'll never forget the time,
When He came to dwell the second time.

We'll never forget the time,
When He came to dwell one thousand years.

No. 98—PEACE OF.

There is a love that comes from God,
Which gives us peace of mind.

There is a love that comes from God,
To lead mankind the way.

There is a love that comes from God,
To unite mankind as one.

There is a love that comes from God,
Which is to all mankind.

No. 99—RALLY AROUND.

Rally around the flag, boys, rally once again,
To protect the land from the foreigner.

Rally around the flag, boys, rally once again,
To protect the land of the free and brave.

Rally around the flag, boys, rally once again,
To protect the land of the Red, White and Blue.

Rally around the flag, boys, rally once again,
To protect the land where the Saviour dwells.

Rally around the flag, boys, rally once again,
To protect the land as God Commands.

No. 100—O, DON'T.

O don't be discouraged, O don't be forlorn,
For the Saviour has come to cheer the world along.

O don't be discouraged, O don't be forlorn,
For He has come to unite us as one.

O don't be discouraged, O don't be forlorn,
For He has come to prolong our days.

O don't be discouraged, O don't be forlorn,
And save up your money at twenty to one.

O don't be discouraged, O don't be forlorn,
And make a home on earth as God commands.

No. 101—TIMES WILL.

Times will now revive, good times will soon be here,
For the Saviour has come to cheer the world along.

Times will now revive, good times will soon be here,
For the Saviour has come to unite us as one.

Times will now revive, good times will soon be here,
For the Saviour has come to prolong our days.

Times will now revive, good times will soon be here,
For the Saviour has come to coin the money twenty to one.

Times will now revive, good times will soon be here,
For the Saviour has come to dwell one thousand years.

No. 102—I LOVE.

I love silver, O how I love gold,
For God has made them for man's own purpose.

I love silver, O how I love gold,
For God has made them for man's own desire.

I love silver, O how I love gold,
For God has made them for man's own comfort.

I love silver, O how I love gold,
For God has made them for man's own pleasure.

I love silver, O how I love gold,
For God has made them for man's own happiness.

I love silver, O how I love gold,
For God has made them to remove the land.

I love silver, O how I love gold,
For God has made them to help save mankind.

No. 103—BEAUTIFUL HOME.

Beautiful home, beautiful home, beautiful home,
Which is here on earth.

Beautiful home, beautiful home, beautiful home,
Which unites us as one.

Beautiful home, beautiful home, beautiful home,
Which prolongs our days.

Beautiful home, beautiful home, beautiful home,
Which is a gift from God.

Beautiful home, beautiful home, beautiful home,
Which is to all mankind.

No. 104—O REJOICE.

O rejoice, O rejoice,
And unite as one.

O rejoice, O rejoice,
And prolong your days.

O rejoice, O rejoice,
And help remove the land.

O rejoice, O rejoice,
And help save mankind.

No. 105—O, BOYS.

O, boys and girls, the Saviour's come.
Come and meet Him now.

O, boys and girls, the Saviour's come.
Come and meet Him in the flold.

O, boys and girls, the Saviour's come.
Come and accept God's great plan.

O, boys and girls, the Saviour's come.
Come and learn of Him the way.

No. 106—COME IN.

O come in the fold and receive the love of God
While the Saviour is here.

O come in the fold and receive the love of God
To cheer us on our way.

O come in the fold and receive the love of God
To unite us as one.

O come in the fold and receive the love of God
To prolong our days.

No. 107—O. COME.

O come and unite with Jesus,
To lead mankind the way.

O come and unite with Jesus,
To march the world along.

O come and unite with Jesus,
To prolong our days.

O come and unite with Jesus,
And help remove the land.

O come and unite with Jesus,
And help save mankind.

No. 108—JUDGMENT.

O the judgment day has come,
The Saviour's on earth to dwell.

O the judgment day has come,
The Saviour's among men.

O the judgment day has come,
He is to judge all mankind.

Yes, the judgment day has come,
The Saviour's with mankind to dwell.

Yes, the judgment day has come,
The Saviour's with mankind to stay.

Yes, the judgment day has come,
He's come to lead mankind the way.

No. 109—JUST THE.

Come, people, see Him here on earth,
It's just the same Saviour.

Except the plan that God has laid,
It's just the same Saviour.

For it was laid by God's command,
It's just the same Saviour.

No. 110—MANY WAITING.

O, children, there is many waiting
To meet the Saviour once more.

O, children, there is many waiting
To meet Him in God's great throne.

O, children, there is many waiting
To meet Him in God's great shore.

Some children has left their earthly homes,
And will not meet the Saviour to-day.

But sometime the Saviour will return
Then they will meet Him on God's great shore.

Let us walk, let us walk with the Saviour,
While He is here on earth.

Let us walk, let us walk with the Saviour,
For we will meet Him in God's great throne.

Let us walk, let us walk with the Saviour,
For He will meet us on God's great shore.

No. 111—CHILDREN'S.

God's great day has come,
The Saviour has arrived,
The children coming home
To meet him in the fold,
And learn of Him the way.
O glory, glory to his name.

God's great day has come,
The Saviour has arrived,
The children coming home
To meet him in the fold,
And learn of God's great day.
O glory, glory to His name.

God's great day has come,
The Saviour has arrived,
The children coming home

To meet him in the fold,
And except God's great plan.
O glory, glory to His name.

No. 112—THE LOVE.

The love, the love, such wonderful, wonderful love,
That we now enjoy since Jesus came to dwell.

The love, the love, such beautiful, beautiful love,
That we now enjoy since Jesus came to stay,

The love, the love, such glorious, glorious love
That we now enjoy since Jesus came to roam.

No. 113—O MYRTLE.

O Myrtle, my sweet darling girl,
Are you without a home in this world?
One has come from a bright, bright shore,
To dwell on earth one thousand years,
One has come from a bright, bright shore,
To make this world a world of love.

O Myrtle, my sweet darling girl,
Are you without a home in this world.
One has come from a bright, bright shore,
To make this world a world as one.
One has come from a bright, bright shore,
To make this world a home for man.

O Myrtle, my sweet darling girl,
Are you without a home in this word?
There will be a time on this land
That you will have a home with me.
There will be a time on this land
That you and I will dwell at home.

No. 114—O. WONDERFUL.

O wonderful love, O wonderful love.
O what wonderful love that comes from God,
Since Jesus come to lead mankind the way.

O wonderful love, O wonderful love.
O what wonderful love that comes from God,
Since Jesus come to unite mankind as one.

O wonderful love, O wonderful love.
O what wonderful love that comes from God,
Since Jesus come to prolong our days.

O wonderful love. O wonderful love.
O what wonderful love that comes from God,
Since Jesus come to remove the land.

No. 115—O LET'S.

O let's all join with the Saviour,
And make this world a world of peace.
O let's all join with the Saviour
And make this world a world of joy.
O let's all join with the Saviour
And make this world a world of love.

No. 116—THERE ONLY.

There's only one way to civilize mankind,
And that is to join the Saviour's band.
There's only one way to civilize mankind,
And that is to join the Saviour's church.
There's only one way to civilize mankind,
And that is to accept God's great plan.

No. 117—BY THE.

By the will of the world the Saviour should dwell.
By the will of the world the Saviour should rule.
By the will of the word the Saviour should reign.
To divide the high sea.
To remove the land.
To save mankind.

No. 118—O LOVE.

O love the children. O love the children,
For its God's design.
O love the children. O love the children.

GREETINGS.

For its God's own command.
O love the children, O love the children,
For its God's great plan.

O, meet the Saviour, O, meet the Saviour,
For its God's design.
O, meet the Saviour, O, meet the Saviour,
For its God's own command.
O, meet the Saviour, O, meet the Saviour,
For its God's great plan.

No. 119—O, UNITE.

O, unite with the Saviour.
O, unite with the Saviour.
For He has come to stay.
O, unite with the Saviour.
O, unite with the Saviour.
To lead mankind the way.

O, unite with the Saviour.
O, unite with the Saviour.
For He has come to dwell.
O, unite with the Saviour.
O, unite with the Saviour.
To save mankind as well.

No. 120—LET'S MAKE.

Let's make this world a world of love.
And join the Saviour's church.
Let's make this world a world of joy,
And join the Saviour's band.
Let's make this world a world of peace,
And unite mankind as one.

No. 121—LET'S.

Let's make this world as God designs.
And remove the land to high sea.
Let's make this world as God commands.
And remove the land to the high sea.
Let's make this world on God's great plan.
And remove the land to the high sea.

No. 122—O, YOU.

O you Zion, O you Zion, let's join hands as God designs,
O you Zion, O you Zion, let's join hands as God commands.
O you Zion, O you Zion, let's join hands and unite as one.
O you Zion, O you Zion, let's join hands and remove the land.
O you Zion, O you Zion, let's join hands and save mankind.

No. 123—O MERLEY.

O Merley, O my sweet little girl,
You are as sweet as any flower.
If you will unite with me
We will soar on the wings of love,
And fly to the shores of Galilee.

O Merley, O my sweet little girl,
You are as sweet as any flower.
If you will unite with me
We will soar on the wings of love,
And sail across the ocean deep.

O Merley, O my sweet little girl,
You are as sweet as any flower.
If you will unite with me
We will soar on the wings of love,
And land upon the other shore.

No. 124—THERE'S A.

There's a land that is fairer than day.
Of which the Saviour of man once dwelt.
There's a land that is fairer than day,
Of which the Saviour of man has left.
And come to the earth to unite us as one.

There's a land that is fairer than day,
Of which the saviour of man once dwelt.
There's a land that is fairer than day,
Of which the Saviour of man has left.
And come to earth to prolong our days.

No. 125—SOME SAY.

Some say that the Saviour sells books just for the coin,
When the people tremble under His voice.
And the world weeps over His songs.
Will they then say that the Saviour
Just sells books for the coin?

No. 126—O KATIE.

O Katie, I have come home to meet you again,
Do you remember the plains where we once roamed?
And on one bright sunshiny day
When we sat under the bough of a tree
And talked of uniting as one?

Did you know that it has been two thousand years
Since the time we dwelt on the plains?
And since the days that we once roamed
Did you know that it has been two thousand years?

Since we sat under the bough of a tree
And talked of uniting as one.

I have often thought of you when I was all alone.
I have often thought of the plains where we once roamed.
I have often thought of the time
When we talked of uniting as one.

O, Katie, I have come from a bright, bright shore
To meet you on land and unite as one
I have come from a bright, bright shore,
To visit the plains where we once roamed.

O, Katie, when will we unite as one?
And talk of the days that has now gone by?
O, Katie, when will we unite as one
And visit the plains where we once roamed.

This is a second time that I have come
To meet you on land and unite as one.
This is a second time that I have come
To visit the plains where we once roamed.

O Katie, there is a bright, bright shore,
Where we will some time meet again.
O Katie, there is a bright, bright shore,
Where we will some time roam.
O Katie, there is a bright, bright shore,
Where we will some time unite again.

No. 127—YOUNG PEOPLE.

O come, come, come to the Saviour,
And see Him here on earth.
O come, come, come to the Saviour,
And see Him face to face.

O come, come, come to the Saviour,
And cheer Him on the way.
O come, come and dwell with the Saviour
And see Him as He is.

O come, come and dwell with the Saviour
And learn of Him the way.
O come and dwell with the Saviour,
And learn of God's great day.

O come, come and meet with the Saviour,
And see Him here on earth.
O come, come and meet with the Saviour,
And see Him face to face.
Yes, come, come and meet the Saviour,
And cheer Him on the way.

No. 128—REPLY.

O, Saviour, we have come to meet you,
And see you face to face.
O, Saviour, we have come to meet you,
And see you here on earth.
O, Saviour, we have come to meet you,
And cheer you on your way.

Yes, Saviour, we have come to dwell with thee,
And see you as you are.
Yes, Saviour, we have come to dwell with thee,

And learn of you the way.
Yes, Saviour, we have come to dwell with thee,
And learn of God's great day.

O, Saviour, we have now met you,
And saw you face to face.
O, Saviour, we have now met you,
And saw you here on earth.
Yes, Saviour, we have now met you,
We cheer you on your way.

No. 129—MAGGIE.

O Maggie, dear Maggie, sweet Maggie, dear,
I have come home to meet you again.
It has been so lonely without you.

O Maggie, dear Maggie, sweet Maggie, dear,
I have brought you good news.
Such news prolongs your days.

O Maggie, dear Maggie, sweet Maggie, dear.
When will we unite as one?
And help to save mankind?

No. 130—O. SAVIOUR.

O Saviour, dear Saviour, sweet Saviour, dear,
I am so glad that you have come to meet me again.
I have been so lonely without you.

O Saviour, dear Saviour, sweet Saviour, dear.
I thank God for such a noble gift.
We will now unite as one,
And help to save mankind.

No. 131—THERE'S A.

There's a land that is fairer than day,
Of which the Saviour of man once dwelt.
One dear friend has left its home
And dwells in God's great throne.
One dear friend has left its home,
And dwells on God's great shore.

There's a land that is fairer than day,
Of which the Saviour of man once dwelt,
One dear friend has left its home
It now dwells in peace with God.
One dear friend has left its home
It now dwells on the other shore.

O glory, when will the Saviour return?
O glory, when will the Saviour come home?
O glory, when will He come to meet us again?

No. 132—O, O, O.

O, O, O, chow, chow, chow,
Melican man's God has come.
O, O, O, Him comee me;
Chow, chow, chow, I comee Him.
O, O, O. Him telee me
When I die eat ricee all the same.
O, O, O, Him not much eatee.
Chow, chow, chow, Him not muchee read.
O, O, O, chow, chow, chow,
Talk like hellee all the same.

No. 133—GOD SENT.

God sent the Saviour to unite us as one.
God sent the Saviour to lead us the way.
God sent the Saviour to prolong our days.
God sent the Saviour to remove the land.

No. 134—GOD'S GREAT.

God's great day has come at last,
The old shepherd has arrived.
The old flock has come home,
To meet the old shepherd again.

The old flock has come home
To lie down in the fold.
The old flock has come home

GREETINGS.

To learn of him the way.
The old flock has come home
To learn of God's great day.

No. 135—O FLORA.

O Flora, my sweet Flora, dear,
When will we unite as one.
And turn the world upside down.
When will we unite as one
And fly to the plains of Gallilee?

O Flora, my sweet Flora, dear,
I have crossed the wide ocean
To meet you on this great shore.
When will we unite as one,
And dwell one thousand years?

No. 136—GOD'S GREAT.

God's great day has come.
Some will weep and wail.
In fear and dismay.
We should all rejoice.
For its God's great plan
To unite us as one
And prolong our days.

God's gerat day has come.
Some will weep and wail.
In fear and dismay
We should all rejoice
For its God's great plan
To remove the land,
And to save mankind.

No. 137—O GLORY.

O glory, when we go home.
And land on the other shore.
We will meet our friends
Who we have met before.

GREETINGS.

O glory, when we go home.
And land on the other shore.
We'll dwell on land where God we'll see.

No. 138—THIS WORLD.

This world was made for mankind to dwell,
This world was made as a home for man.
This world was made for mankind ot dwell in peace and love
This world was made for mankind to dwell one thousand years.
This world was made for mankind to rule without war.

No. 139—O MASSA.

O massa, O massa,
We have come to meet you too.

O massa, O massa,
We have come to lie down in the fold.

O massa, O massa,
We have come to learn of you the way.

O massa, O massa,
We have come to learn of God's great day.

No. 140—O WHAT.

O what did Christ do in this world?
In the way of uniting mankind,
And prolonging their days?
O what did Christ do in this world,
In the way of removing the land,
To make a home for man?

O Jesus has laid the great plan,
By the hand of His Maker's request,
In the way of uniting mankind,
And prolonging their days.

O Jesus has laid the great plan,
By the hand of His Maker's request,
In the way of removing the land,
To make a home for man.

No. 141—EDNA.

O, my dear sweetheart, O my sweetheart, dear,
When will we soar on wings of love
And reach the land of corn and wine?
When will we soar on wings of love
And fly to the plains of Gallilee.

O, my dear sweetheart, O my sweetheart, dear,
I have loved you with all my heart,
For many long and lonely years.
When will we soar on wings of love
And roam on the plains once more?

No. 142—REPRESENTATION.

O what is that rumbling?
It's the Saviour of man.
He's left God's throne,
And coming to the land
To save mankind.

Let's leave our tombs
And meet Him too.
Let's leave our tombs
And meet Him on land.
O Saviour, we have left our tombs.
We have left our tombs
To meet you on land.

No. 143—MY NATIVE.

My native land, the land on which the pilgrims dwelt,
The land on which the pilgrims fought and freed.

My native land, the land of which the brave boys,
Made England say I have enough of thee.

The land to which the nation made Chile bend the knee,
The land of which the brave boys made Spain say
I have enough too.

My native land, the land in which a Saviour dwells,
The land of liberty, the land of the free.
I love thee now, I love thee still.

They are the patriotic ones,
They are the patriotic boys,
Who made England say I want no more.

They are the patriotic ones,
They are the patriotic boys
Who made Chile bend the knee.

They are the patriotic ones,
They are the patriotic boys,
Who made Spain say that will do.

They are the patriotic ones,
They are the patriotic boys,
Who freed this great land of ours.

No. 144—OUR HEADS.

Our heads are turning gray.
Our limbs are growing weak.
We will not have long to stay.
We thank God for sending the Saviour
To lead mankind the way.
O glory, glory to Its name.

Our heads are turning gray.
Our limbs are growing weak.
We will not have long to stay.
We thank God for sending the Saviour
To make a home for man.
O glory, glory to Its name.

Our heads are turning gray,
Our limbs are growing weak.
We soon will return and dwell in God's great throne.
We will then look for the Saviour to return.
O glory, glory to His name.

We soon will return and dwell on God's great shore.
When we have been there one thousand years.
The Saviour will return and meet us again.
O glory, glory to His name.

No. 145—WE WILL.

We will no more look for the Saviour,
For He's with us to-day;
Let us now rejoice with him,
As we see him face to face.

O rejoice, now rejoice,
O rejoice with him.
O rejoice, now rejoice,
As we met him to-day.

No. 146—O LOVE.

O love the Saviour, O love the Saviour,
Such love I never endured.

O love the Saviour, O love the Saviour,
Such love I never enjoyed.

O love the Saviour, O love the Saviour,
Such love comes from God.

O love the Saviour, O love the Saviour,
Such love is to all mankind.

No. 147—HAPPY.

Happy day, happy day,
The Saviour's with us here to stay.
Happy day, happy day,
He leads us by the hand to-day.

Happy day, happy day,
He has now come with us to stay.
Happy day, happy day,
He has now come with us to stay.

No. 148—WE ARE.

We are going home, we are going home,
We are going home to God's great throne.

We are going home, we are going home,
We are going home to unite again.

We are going home, we are going home,
We are going home to dwell with God.

When the Saviour comes, when the Saviour comes,
When the Saviour comes He'll meet us there.
When the Saviour comes, when the Saviour comes,
When the Saviour comes He'll dwell with us.
When the Saviour comes, when the Saviour comes,
When the Saviour comes , He'll lead us there.

We are going home, we are going home,
We are going home to dwell with God.
When we get there and unite as one,
We'll then thank God for righteousness.
When we get there and unite as one
We'll then thank God for such a place.

No. 149—O LET.

O let the Saviour dwell,
For it's God's will.

O let the Saviour rule,
For it's God's design.

O let the Saviour reign.
For it's God's command.

No. 150—THE GREAT.

The great shepherd has come.
He has come to gather His flock to His fold,
When they hear His voice they will know Him.
And will heed to His call,
And come and lie down at His feet in the fold.

No. 151—A VOICE FROM PECK'S BAD BOY.

Ho, ho, ho, I would hate to be in the Saviour's shoes.
To think I had two mothers
And no earthly fathers.

No. 152—REPLY TO PECK'S BAD BOY.

Ho, ho, ho, I would hate to be in your shoes,
To think I only had one mother,
And didn't know who my father was.

No. 153—SALVATION ARMY.

March through the cities
With a banner of five stars
And a great big drum.
And sing the Saviour's songs.
Every once and a while cry out,
Who will flip a dollar on the drum?
I would like to see how it would sound,
And when the sister goes around
With the tambourine,
She can walk back to the captain and say,
See what God has done for me.
And when you go home and lie down to rest,
You can rejoice over such earthly gifts.

No. 154—THERE WAS.

There was a time when the Saviour of man.
Dwelt on the plains of Galilee.
And at that time God laid the plan
To lead mankind the way.

No. 155—WHEN

When snakes travel on land
As swift as any grayhound.
Will mankind then ignore
God's great millenium day?

No. 156—DEAR.

Dear Negroes and Indians, I have come to you
To teach you the way that God designs.
It's God's design, not mine.
That you no longer with the white man dwell.

I love you, I wish you well.
It's God's design that you give up the land.
O believe me and receive me.
For I receive you.

Gentle Saviour, gentle Saviour,
We have come to meet you.
We also receive you.
We don't blame you
For teaching us the way.

If it's God's command that we no longer
With the white man dwell.
And God's design that we give up the land.
We shall depart and give up the land
At the white man's command.

No. 157—ACROSS THE OCEAN.

The Saviour of man is on earth.
Yes, He is here. I read it the other day.
And they say it's true.
Yes, He's the old Saviour
That dwelt here before.

O how glad I would be to meet Him,
And take Him by the hand.
And see the old, old Saviour
That was here before.

O how glad I would be to meet Him.
And dwell by His side.
And ask about the land
That's beyond death's door.

And learn of Him when He intends to cross
The wide ocean and dwell with us here.

No. 158—TO THE PRISONERS.

Prison punishment is contrary to God's will.
And should be abolished as soon as possible.
By a legal process of law.

Enacted by the porper authorities of the nations
The governors of the different states.

With the union of the United States of America
Should release prisoners to the fullest extent,
That the law provides.
This also applies to officers of all nations
That has the pardoning power.

No. 159—THIS IS.

This is a second time
The Saviour has come
To set aside the Jewish bible.

This is a second time
The Saviour has come
To receive the Jewish people.

Will they now receive Him?
Or will they reject Him
At this second call?

No. 160—PAPA.

Papa, papa, papa, dear,
Whose daughter am I?
Daughter, you are a child of a king.
I thank God for such a gift.

Well, papa, if I am a child of a king
I thank God for righteousness.
Daughter, you should thank God.
For mamma and sister, dear.

O, mamma dear, did you know
That I was a child of a king:
Yes, daughter, you are a child
Of the great, great King.

I thank God for such a gift.
You should thank God for Papa too.
Mamma, I do thank God for papa.
And mamma and sister, dear.

No. 161—REPLY TO AN OLD DOCTOR.

O doctor, doctor, dear, you old bald head,
I have come to you.
I have come to teach you your A B C.
Yes, dear doctor, come to me now,
And I will teach you how to do.

Yes, dear doctor, come and see,
And I will teach you how to be
Be as God would have you be.
Do as God would have you do, and receive me.
Then you can say your A B C and E F G.

No. 162—REPLY TO A FOOL.

You old snotagoslir and stealtrap gin,
I have come to you.
I have come to teach you how to do.

When money was left in your hands
By one who was honest and true,
You should have delivered it
As he told you to do.
Then the neighbors would not have said
That you was dishonest and untrue.

Whenyou swindle your neighbor
Out of his just due,
Remember that God was right
When It sent a Saviour to teach you how to do.

If you had your just dues as the law provides,
You would be peeping through the bars.
The same as any who do.

No. 163—POP.

Pop, pop, pop, hear those guns.
Pop, pop, pop, hear those cannon.
Boom, boom, boom, hear those shells.

Well, I'll be dog goned,
The Saviour was right,
The war has begun.

No. 164—THOSE THAT.

God has said to the Saviour of man,
In the year ten thousand and one.

Enough has been done to lay my plan,
Mankind should begin to unite as one,
To make this world a home for man,
Or a great famine will visit the land,
Sent by the will of my own command.

No. 165—McKINLEY.

President, thank God.
That you was the leader
Of the nation at the opening
Of God's great day on earth.

No. 166—CLEVELAND.

Either vote the Republican ticket
Or do away with Republican proclivities.

No. 167—GOVERNOR.

Thank God that you are the leader
Of the mother of the Saviour,
The State of Oregon.

No. 168—POET.

The great poet is coming.
I see Him in God's throne.
I see multitudes of people
Standing around Him.
The tears are flowing down their chees.
As mighty raindrops.
He's coming. See there.
He's landed on the sun.
He is holding God's great banner
In His right hand.
The banner is large enough
To reach around the earth.
There are five stars on the banner

As large as the five continents
He's holding a book in His left hand.
On the back of the book is written,
The Saviour's Bible.
The book is over four
And one-half million years long.
Hear His voice . It roars like a mighty thunder.
It travels like a mighty rushing wind.
See there, He's coming.
He's landed on the earth.
I feel the earth give under my feet.
See those acean waves dash high in the air.
I see multitudes of people following after Him.
I see both the rich and poor falling at Hies feet.
I see the geat physician lie down at His feet.
This is a day of wonders, a day of love.

No. 169—THE.

The Saviour has come at last.
He has come to divide the high sea,
At the will of His maker's request.

Let us all join with Him
And help divide the high sea,
And help divide the great high sea.

No. 170—THIS IS.

This is a second time
The Saviour has dwelt with man.
He has come with us to stay,
And lead the way to Paradise.
O glory, glory to His name.

No. 171—COME, BOYS.

Come, boys and girls, come this way,
For I love you all the day.
Come, boys and girls, come just now,
And I will teach you how to do.

Come, boys and girls, come just now,
And I will teach you how to be,
Be as your parents would have you be,
Do as your parents would have you do.
And don't forget to remember me.

Yes, boys and girls, if you desire
To raise mankind higher and higher.
You must depend on God's command.

God alone can lay the plan.
God alone can raise mankind.
You can see in this book
The great, great plan that God has took.

No. 172—BOYS AND GIRLS REPLY.

Saviour, we have come to meet you.
We have come to receive you.
We have come by God's command.

To see you on God's great land,
We have come to accept the great, great plan
That God has made to save mankind.

No. 173—WHAT WILL.

What will mankind say,
In this God's great day,
When the world is subdued,
And the land stained with blood?
Will they then still say
This is not God's great day?
Or will they accept God's plan
And help remove the land
To make a home for man?
As God designed
From the creation of mankind.

No. 174—WHEN.

When the hail and rain beat the brow of man.
And destroyed the fruit and grain.
Sent by the wrath of God.

In midsummer days.
Then will mankind not say.
This must be God's great day.

No. 175—WHEN THE.

When the meteors fall from the skies,
As a mighty storm at sea,
What will then mankind say,
Concerning this great millenium day.

No. 176—WHEN CROCKODILES.

When crockodiles dwell on land,
To devour both beast and man,
And locusts come by God's command,
To destroy vegetation on the land,
Will the people then join in one great band,
And help remove the land,
To make a home for man?

No. 177—IF THE.

If the people of Marquams, some of those times,
Wake up with a great famine in the land,
Will they then persecute the saviour of man.
And continue the famine in the land?
It's not God's design to strike down mankind.
But it's part of God't great plan,
To protect the Saviour of man.
If it must be done,
Many will fall to save one.
If the Saviour of man is put to death,
The world will be stricken with a great pest.

No. 178—WHEN THE.

When the day of plagues arrive,
Will mankind unite as one,
And take the Saviour by the hand.
And join in one great band?
And help remove the land,
To save all mankind?

GREETINGS.

No. 179—WHEN.

When desolation has come,
And mankind begin to mourn,
Will they then reject God's great plan,
And refuse to remove the land,
And bring destruction to mankind?

No. 180—THOSE THAT.

Those that receive the Saviour of man
Are God's favored people.
Those that reject the Saviour of man
Are like sheep gone astray.
And ignores God's great plan,
Which was sent to the land,
To save mankind.

No. 181—O, DEWEY.

O Dewey, sound the trumpet,
For the Saviour of man has come
O Dewey, sound the trumpet.
He's come to dwell one thousand years.
O Dewey, sound the trumpet.
To unite this nation as one,
And help to divide the high sea.
Yes, to help to divide the great high sea.

No. 182—IF THE.

If the world ignore God's great plan.
And reject the Saviour of man,
Destruction will come upon the land.
And destroy all mankind.

No. 183—THE CHICKENS.

Cackle, cackle, cakle, who's that there?
Cackle, cackle, cackle, I'll be dog goned
If it isn't that old Saviour who was here before.

Cackle, cackle, cackle, O my how I hate Him,
For He loves yellow-legged chickens.

But it's when they are in the pot,
And then sliced up and cooked well done.

They had me saved for a preacher
But the old preacher died,
So I thought I would be left,
But there comes that darned old Saviour.
So I know my name is Dennis.

No. 184—THE DUCK.

Quack, quack, quack, who's that a coming?
Quack, quack, quack, who is he?
Quack, quack, quack, it's the old Saviour.
Quack, quack, quack, He's a lover of ducks.

But it's when they are in the pot and then sliced up
He's worse than a preacher on use ducks.
If He can't get any one to cook them,
He'll eat guts, feathers and all.

No. 185—NEW COON.

New coon in town,
The Saviour of man
Has made a second call.
He has come to stay,
To lead mankind the way.

He has come to dwell,
To save mankind as well.
It's the same old coon
That was in Gallilee
Two thousand years ago.

No. 186—TOM CATS.

The devil and Tom Walker,
If that old cuss hasn't come back.
He loves cats, but it's when they are out of sight.

I am scared half to death,
I hardly know what to do.
There is only one thing we can do.

When we see Him coming is to hide behind a box
And when His back is turned
Run like a cared wolf.

No. 187—WHIPPOWILL.

Wippowill Tipacanoe,
The Saviour's come to us too.
Wippowill Tipacanoe,
He loves us as well as you.
Wippowill Tipacanoe,
He is our Saviour too.

No. 188—THE OWL.

Who, who, who are you?
I'm the boss over all birds.
Who, who, who are you?
I'm the Saviour of man.
Who, who, who the devil you say.

Well then I'm the Saviour of chickens,
So am I, so that's makes me two Saviours,
And you but one.

No. 189—THE JACK AND REPLY.

Oh, oh, oh, what is that? O it's another jackass.
Dear old jackass, as you have been so kind,
I'll give you a rhyme.

I'll take the first name
And give you the last,
And you will still be nothing.
But an old ass.

And they will call me Jack.
And when they hear you bray,
Some one will say, O what is that?
O it's nothing but that old ass.

No. 190—THE DOGS.

Bow, wow, wow, what's that noise?
Bow, wow, wow, I don't know.
Bow, wow, wow, it's some man.

Bow, wow, wow, we'll bite him.
Bow, wow, wow, he draws nigh.
Bow, wow, wow, it's the Saviour of man.

Bow, wow, wow, He loves us.
Bow, wow, wow, we love him.
Bow, wow, wow, let him in.

No. 191—THE LION.

See the great lion a coming.
It's left God's great throne.
It's a coming to the land
To devour mankind.

O no, it's the Saviour of man.
He has come to remove the land.
And make a home for man.

No. 192—THE TADPOLE.

I am nothing but a little tadpole,
And I live in the water
The other day I heard something go kerwhack.

And I looked up and behold it was the Saviour.
He had landed in the water.
I walked up to Him and put my arm around Him.

And I gave Him a big hug,
And said, Dear Saviour, I am so glad
That you have come to purify the water.

No. 193—THE CROW.

I'm an old crow, blacker than any nigger O.
I can sing and hop and dance worse than any nigger O.

I'm an old crow, blacker than any nigger O.
I can sing and hop and dance for the Saviour O.

GREETINGS.

No. 194—THE.

The Saviour of man has come,
I would like to see Him.
When he calls little children
Like lambs to His fold.

I would like to see Him
When He says,
Let the little ones
Come unto me.

No. 195—THE PARROT.

The Saviour of man has come.
Where will priesthood dwell?
Where will infidelity land?

What will the king say,
When they learn that kingdoms
Can no longer stand, oh men.

No. 196—WHY.

Why does some persecute the Saviour of man?
When God freed this great land.
To protect the Saviour of man?

No. 197—THOSE THAT.

Those that persecute the Saviour of man
Is a traitor to this free land,
And ignored God's great plan
Which was made to save mankind.

No. 198—O THE.

O the blood, O the blood
That the pilgrims spilt.
It was spilt to free this land.
It was split for the Saviour of man.

O the blood, O the blood
That the pilgrims spilt.

It was spilt to lay God's plan.
It was spilt to save mankind.

No. 199—THE SAVIOUR.

The Saviour has the right,
The same as any man,
To dwell on this free land.

The Saviour has the right,
The same as any man,
To set forth God's great plan.

The Saviour has the right,
The same as any man,
To unite the world as one.

No. 200—JUDGE MARQUAM.

Judge Marquam is the man
Who built the Marquam Grand,
To help civilize mankind.

No. 201—THE OREGONIAN.

Why not the Oregonian say.
The Saviour has come to stay?
Let's all join in one great band,
And help remove the land
To make this world a home for man.

No. 202—A BANKER.

A banker said, Well, I be dang,
The Saviour is just the man.
He has come to join our band,
And coin the money, twenty to one.

No. 203—WHAT RIGHT.

What right has the physicians to say
That we cannot dwell one thousand years.
When God never said unto them
The water is not composed of small germs.
Of which to destroy the life of man.

No. 204—ROLL ON.

Roll on, boys, the Saviour has come.
He has come by God's command.

Roll on, boys, the Saviour has come,
He has come to lay God's plan.

Roll on, boys, the Saviour has come,
He has come to save mankind.

No. 205—IT'S NO.

It's no use a talking, it's no need to mourn,
For the Saviour has come by God's command.

It's no use a talking, it's no need to mourn,
For He has come to lay God's plan.

It's no use a talking, it's no need to mourn.
For He has come to save mankind.

No. 206—IT WILL.

It will not be many days
Until some will say.
The Saviour has come to stay.
To lead mankind the way,
And prolong our days.
O glory, glory to His name.

No. 207—THE OLD.

The old flock is coming home,
To lie down in the fold.

The old flock is coming home,
To learn of Him the way.

The old flock is coming home,
To learn of God's great day.

No. 208—WHAT WILL.

What will mankind say,
When they learn the great king has come to stay.

To conduct this great millenium day.
And when pestilences compass the land,
To prove that he was sent by God's command.

No. 209—O THE.

O the bible, the bible, the blessed bible,
Which was composed by the Saviour of man.

O the bible, the bible, the blessed bible,
Which was wrote to lay God's plan.

O the bible, the bible, the blessed bible.
Which was wrote to save mankind.

No. 210—GOLD BUG.

I am a gold bug.
I would not be a silver bug
Like the Saviour of man.

No. 211—REPLY.

I am a silver bug,
And a gold bug too.
So I am two bugs,
And you are but one.

No. 212—DO YOU.

Do you know what this book was written for?
It was composed by the Saviour of man,
Of which to lay God's great plan,
To unite all mankind
In one great band,
To remove the land
And make a home for man.

No. 213—Bryan.

Some say the Saviour
Is a brother to Bryan
On the silver question.
He is not a brother.

But you might
Call him a cousin,
For Bryan believes in silver
At the ratio of 16 to 1
In the U. S. only.
The Saviour believes in silver
At the ratio of 20 to 1
The world over.

No. 214—O THE.

O the old ship of Zion has returned.
O who will come aboard.
And soar on the wings of love,
And sail across the ocean deep?
Who will come aboard
And soar on wings of love,
And fly to the plains of Gallilee?

No. 215—WHAT HAS.

What has priesthood done,
To unite the world as one,
And remove the land,
To make a home for man.

Jesus has laid the great plan
To unite the world as one,
And remove the land
To make a home for man.

No. 216—THE GOVERNMENT.

The Saviour of man has come
To prolong our days.
Don't make any more life time donation
Except in case of necessity.
Let me put a flea in your ear,
There is twenty ounces of silver
To one of gold in the earth,
And the U. S. owns a large portion of it.
Put 350 grains of silver in a dollar,

Pay off the old debt by the old gold weight.
Then you can make other nations
Say enough, enough,
We will have to coin our money
Of the same stuff, stuff.

No. 217—DEWEY.

My name is Dewey,
I am one of the brave boys
That the Saviour mentioned in His bible.
I hope some day to meet Him.
Then I will greet Him
For using such noble words of honor.

No. 218—IF KINGS.

If kings do not give up their thrones,
To help unite mankind as one,
Great tribulation will visit their lands,
Sent by the will of God's own command.

No. 219—THE U. S.

Hush, little baby, don't you cry,
Because Oregon is the mother of the Saviour.
Remember that Oregon is within the Union;
So you are the mother of the Saviour, too.

No. 220—GOD.

God's great day has come, O glory.
God's great day has come, O glory.

Glory to Its name.
Glory to Its name.

No. 221—THE.

The Saviour's come.
The Saviour's come.

We welcome Him
We welcome Him
To His fold.

Halleluiah, praise God.
Halleluiah, prainse God.

No. 222—IF.

If Christianity is right,
Why has not mankind united
Before the second coming
Of the Saviour of man.

No. 223—IF.

If mankind will unite as one,
And help remove the land,
There will be no pestilence.
Visit the land sent by God's command.

No. 224—SOME.

Some may say Marquam is crazy,
The land can never be removed.
But if God sends a great famine
And when many shout O glory,
Will they then say Marquam is crazy?
Or will they unite as one,
And help mae a home for man.

No. 225—IF THE.

If the world is wise,
And Marquam is crazy,
Whay has not mankind
United as one and made
This world a home for man.
Before Marquam dwelt on land?

No. 226—IS IT.

Is it possible that a crazy man
Could have laid this plan
To unite the world as one
And remove the land
To make a home for man.

No. 227—IF.

If Marquam is a fool,
And earthly physicians know it all,
Why do their heads go bald
And their eyes soon fail.
And they lie down and die
Without knowing why.

No. 228—THE REASON.

The reasons some physicians may say
Marquam is insane
Is because this great plan
Will heal the diseases of man.
And take the patient
Right out of their own hands.

No. 229—IF.

If Marquam is insane,
Could he compose one song.
To cheer the world along?
Could he compose so many songs.
To lay God's great plan
To remove the land
To make a home for man?
When the world is not so wise.
To comprehen the plan,
To remove the land.
And make a home for man.

All communications should be addressed to
PHILIP A. MARQUAM,
Oregon City, Oregon.

www.ingramcontent.com/pod-product-compliance
Lightning Source LLC
Chambersburg PA
CBHW020121170426
43199CB00009B/580